CHECK OUT this epic shot of the 64,000-capacity Saint Petersburg Stadium at this year's Confederations Cup final. It will host one of the World Cup semi-finals next summer!

Welcome

You can also catch up with MOTD on BBC iPlayer!

Don't forget to keep watching MOTD, readers!

2017 THE FOOTBALL HEADLINES!

LIFT-OFF Gary Cahill and David Luiz hold the Prem trophy aloft!

WHAT A YEAR!

WOW, 2017 WAS packed full of drama, excitement and epic action. In this MOTD mag annual we'll look back at the highs and lows of the last 12 months, as well as looking forward to 2018. Happy reading!

BBC One Don't miss *Match of the Day*, Saturdays and Sundays on BBC One and BBC Two!

HOT-SHOT HARRY AT IT AGAIN!

Tottenham and England striker Harry Kane finished top scorer in the Premier League for the second year in a row!

WEMBLEY JOY FOR WENGER!

Arsenal won the FA Cup for a third time in four years – easing the pressure on their under-fire manager Arsene Wenger!

RONALDO AT THE DOUBLE!

C-Ron netted two to secure back-to-back UCL wins for Spanish champs Real Madrid, as they beat Juventus 4-1 in Cardiff. Boom!

MOUR GLORY FOR JOSE!

Jose Mourinho's Man. United beat Ajax in the final of the Europa League – ensuring they qualify for the Champions League!

NEYMAR

Once upon a time, a cheeky scamp on the streets of Sao Paulo dreamt of becoming... he's the mos...

KINGS CONTE & KANTE!

Chelsea claimed the Premier League title in Antonio Conte's first season at Stamford Bridge – and midfield ace N'Golo Kante was voted PFA Player of the Year!

WATCH LIONEL MESSI... LIVE!

RUSSIA 2018

A IS FOR ARSENAL
B IS FOR BRIAN DEANE
C IS FOR...
D IS FOR DILLY DING, DILLY DONG
E IS FOR ENTERTAINERS
F IS FOR FERGIE TIME

NEYMAR MADNESS!

Incredible scenes as PSG splashed out a world-record £198m to sign Brazilian superstar Neymar from Barcelona. What a signing!

AVOID THIS BOOK IF YOU ARE...

An alpaca
You'll just try to eat it!

A knitting fan
Trust us, it's not for you!

A banana
You can't even read!

30 WAYS TO become a baller!

NEY

Once upon a time, a cheeky scamp on the streets of Sao Paulo dreamt of becoming a footballer – 20 years later he's the most expensive player of all time!

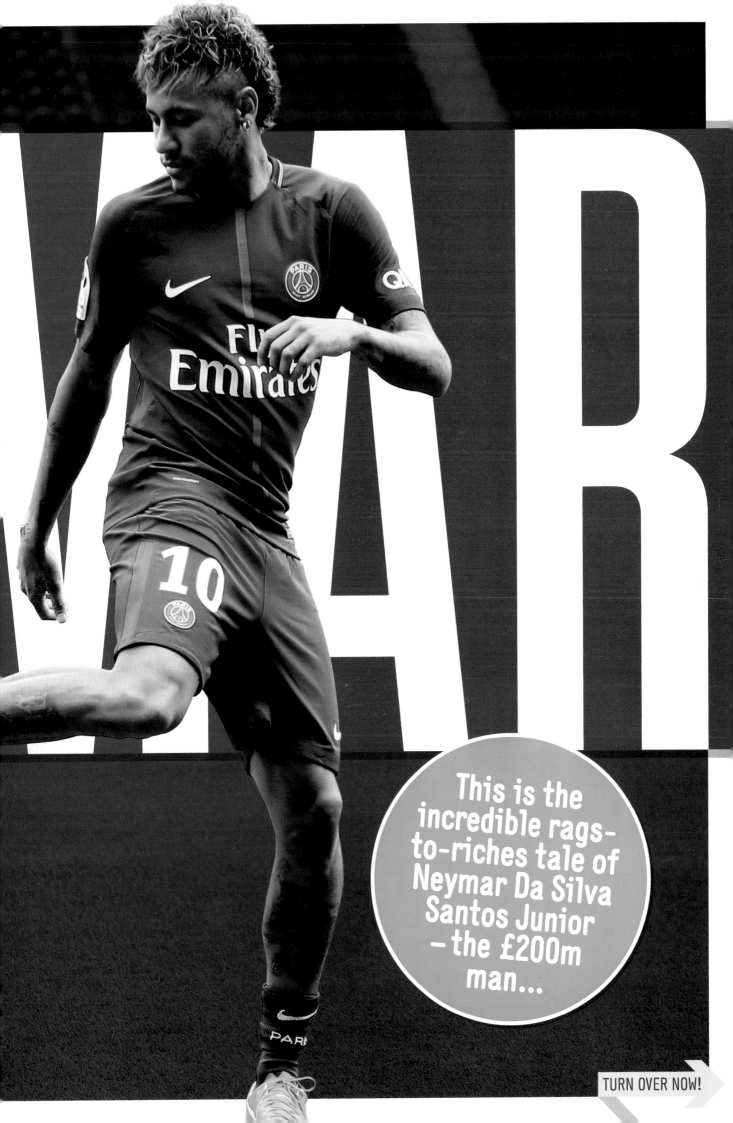

This is the incredible rags-to-riches tale of Neymar Da Silva Santos Junior – the £200m man...

TURN OVER NOW!

The story begins in 1992 in Sao Paulo, Brazil's biggest city...

Neymar Santos senior, a journeyman Brazilian footballer, and his wife Nadine da Silva are celebrating the birth of their baby boy. Little Neymar junior loves football and by the age of 11, he's been signed by Santos, one of Brazil's biggest clubs!

As a 14-year-old, he rejects Real Madrid...

The hype around Neymar is insane – with word of his God-given talent even spreading to the Spanish capital, Madrid. But he stays loyal to his hometown team Santos and finally makes his pro debut in 2009 as a fresh-faced 17-year-old!

A Samba showman is well and truly born...

The kid is an instant star. Santos reject big-money offers from West Ham and Chelsea to keep hold of their local hero – and it's a wise move. Over the next four years he scores a total of 136 goals in 225 games, helping the club win six major trophies as well as gobbling up a load of individual awards!

20 YEARS OF WORLD-RECORD TRANSFERS!

How the world record has changed hands over the past two decades!

1997	1998	1999	2000	2000
RONALDO	DENILSON	CHRISTIAN VIERI	HERNAN CRESPO	LUIS FIGO
BARCELONA TO INTER MILAN	**SAO PAULO TO REAL BETIS**	**LAZIO TO INTER MILAN**	**PARMA TO LAZIO**	**BARCELONA TO REAL MADRID**
£19.5m	£21.5m	£32m	£35.5m	£37m

In May 2013, he waves goodbye to Brazil...

Aged 21, he heads to Europe to join Barcelona for £71.5m, signing a five-year deal with a £190m release clause. After a slow start he turns on the style and over the next four seasons confirms his status as one of the world's best footballers!

It's goals, goals, goals with the MSN...

Following Luis Suarez's move to the Nou Camp in 2014, Neymar, Lionel Messi and Suarez form the most formidable strike force in history. MSN fire Barca to domestic and UCL glory – as well as shattering Spanish goalscoring records!

ALL HAIL THE KING OF BRAZIL!

Neymar is the golden boy of Brazilian footy– and it's not surprising. Since netting on his Brazil debut in 2010, he hasn't stopped scoring – at just 25, he's the country's fourth-highest scorer and has already led them to glory at the 2013 Confederations Cup and the 2016 Olympics!

Then in August 2017, Neymar stuns the world...

After winning eight trophies with Barca, playing in front of 90,000 fans at the Nou Camp and rewriting history with Messi and co, Neymar quits Spain to move to French club PSG for a world-record £200m. Will he live happily ever after?

BRAZIL TOP SCORERS!

	PLAYER	YEARS	GAMES / GOALS
1	Pele	1957-1971	92 / 77
2	Ronaldo	1994-2011	98 / 62
3	Romario	1987-2005	70 / 55
4	Neymar	2010-	77 / 52

2001	2009	2009	2013	2016	2017
ZINEDINE ZIDANE	KAKA	CRISTIANO RONALDO	GARETH BALE	PAUL POGBA	NEYMAR
JUVENTUS TO REAL MADRID	AC MILAN TO REAL MADRID	MAN. UNITED TO REAL MADRID	TOTTENHAM TO REAL MADRID	JUVENTUS TO MAN. UNITED	BARCELONA TO PSG
£46.6m	£56m	£80m	£86m	£89m	£200m

TURN OVER FOR MORE!

The crazy numbers behind the £200m man...

If you wondered why PSG smashed the world transfer record to sign Neymar then these stats should reveal why!

Neymar's all-important stats!

SANTOS

2009-2013

GAMES	GOALS	GOALS PER GAME
225	136	0.6

BARCELONA

2013-2017

GAMES	GOALS	GOALS PER GAME
186	105	0.56

BRAZIL

2010-

GAMES	GOALS	GOALS PER GAME
77	52	0.68

FACT FILE
FULL NAME: Neymar Da Silva Santos Junior
DATE OF BIRTH: 5 February 1992 (age 25)
PLACE OF BIRTH: Mogi Das Cruzes, Brazil
HEIGHT: 5ft 9in **WEIGHT:** 10st 10lb

Neymar's goalscoring record!

SEASON	GOALS	
2010	42	**SANTOS**
2011	24	
2012	43	
2013	13	

SEASON	GOALS	
2013-14	15	**BARCELONA**
2014-15	39	
2015-16	31	
2016-17	20	

MSN RIP 2014-2017...

The best front three in footy history!

2014-15	122 GOALS
2015-16	131 GOALS
2016-17	111 GOALS

His Barcelona highlights!

● Neymar had a hand in 164 goals in 188 games during his time with the Spanish giants, scoring 105 and grabbing 59 assists!

● He won eight trophies in four seasons with Barca – three Copa Del Rey wins, two La Liga titles, a Spanish Super Cup, one UCL and the Club World Cup!

● Neymar was the only player from the top five European leagues with more than 20 goals AND more than 20 assists last season!

THE CHANGING FACE (& HAIR) OF NEYMAR!

 2010

 2011

 2012

 2013

 2014

 2015

 2016

 2017

FOOTY DETECTIVE!

Piece together the evidence and name the leagues...

HOW DID YOU DO? TURN TO p92 FOR THE ANSWERS!

CLUE 1 CLUE 2

HERBALIFE NUTRITION

LEAGUE A

CLUE 3 CLUE 4

NYC FOOTBALL CLUB

WRITE YOUR ANSWER HERE

CLUE 1 CLUE 2

Joma

LEAGUE B

CLUE 3 CLUE 4

WRITE YOUR ANSWER HERE

CLUE 1 CLUE 2

YAMAHA YAMAHA YAMAHA

BBVA

LEAGUE C

CLUE 3 CLUE 4

N O B

WRITE YOUR ANSWER HERE

CLUE 1 CLUE 2

LEAGUE D

CLUE 3 CLUE 4

WRITE YOUR ANSWER HERE

For more quiz action check out bbc.co.uk/cbbc/games

HARRY KANE

Tottenham

POGBA'S PICK 'N' MIX!

Paul Pogba oozes style – here's your chance to dress the superstar just as you want to!

DRESS YOUR OWN POGBA!

Simply cut out The Pog and the items and get dressing!

Fold the white tabs around Pogba's body to secure the clothing!

TOP TIP! Stick Pogba onto a piece of card – then you can stand him up!

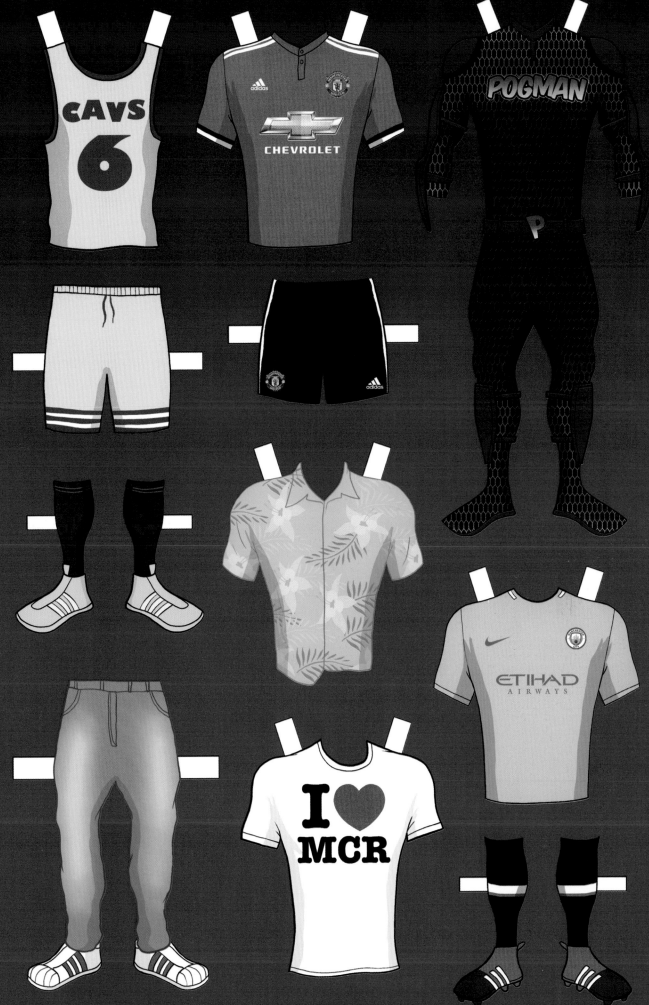

CAVS 6

CHEVROLET

POGMAN

P

ETIHAD
A I R W A Y S

I ♥ MCR

Illustrations: Dan Leydon (danleydon.com)

MARCUS RASHFORD

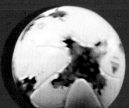

Man. United

20 THINGS TO DO BEFORE YOU'RE 20

The ultimate list for football lovers!

TURN OVER NOW!

1 WATCH LIONEL MESSI... LIVE!

WE KNOW YOU'VE seen him on TV – everyone has. But being in a stadium and seeing him bamboozle and befuddle even the world's best defenders is next level. Players this good only come along once every gazillion years, so figure out how YOU can get to the Nou Camp to watch little Leo in action before he retires!

I DID IT! ✓

GET YOURSELF TO THE WESTFALENSTADION! 2

THE WESTFAL-WHAT? This is the home of German giants Borussia Dortmund – the club with the highest average attendance in the whole of Europe last season. Behind the goal is the monstrous and very yellow Sudtribune, where more than 24,000 super-fans sing, bounce and shout!

I DID IT! ✓

AVERAGE ATTENDANCE 2016-17

1 B. Dortmund 79,653
2 Barcelona 77,944
3 Man. United 75,289
4 Bayern Munich 75,000
5 Real Madrid 69,170

TAKE IN A LOCAL DERBY – IN THE UK! 3

THERE'S NOTHING BETTER than beating your local rivals – but on the flip side, there's nothing worse than losing to them! That's why derby days are absolutely buzzing and simply need to be sampled!

I DID IT! ✓

TOP 5 DERBIES THIS SEASON!

1 Old Firm derby Celtic v Rangers
2 Manchester derby Man. United v Man. City
3 North London derby Arsenal v Tottenham
4 Merseyside derby Liverpool v Everton
5 Second City derby Aston Villa v Birmingham

5

SCORE A PANENKA!

FOR THOSE THAT don't know, a Panenka is when you cheekily chip a penalty down the middle as the keeper dives despairingly to the side. To pull off this ultimate bit of tekkers – the king of pens – you need nerves of steel and supreme confidence!

I DID IT! ✔

Did you know?
The trick is named after Czech star Antonin Panenka. In the Euro 1976 final, he scored the winning penalty with a soft chip!

A B C D E

START A COLLECTION OF FOOTY SHIRTS!

6

IN 20 YEARS' time you'll look back and think – 'Why didn't I buy more football shirts?' And in 20 years' time you'll think football shirts ain't what they used to be. So our tip of the day is to start collecting those shirts NOW. By the year 2037, you'll have a collection fit for a football king!

I DID IT! ✔

TOP 5 SHIRTS OF ALL TIME!

A Saint-Etienne 1980-81
B Holland 1988-89
C West Germany 1988-91
D Sampdoria 1991
E Denmark 1986-87

4

THEN HEAD TO THE BIGGEST OF THE LOT – THE SUPERCLASICO!

TALKING OF DERBIES, they simply don't come any bigger than this. We're in Buenos Aires, the capital of Argentina, and it's the city's two superclubs Boca Juniors and River Plate going head to head. This is not for the squeamish. It's loud, it's intense and it's utterly, utterly off the chart!

I DID IT! ✔

THE HOLIDAY Disneyland Paris! ✔

THE SOUVENIR SHIRT PSG! ✔

7

IN FACT, BUY ONE ON EVERY HOLIDAY!

NOT ONLY WILL you have a wicked memento from every holiday you've been on, but you'll have an awesome collection of shirts from different towns, cities and countries. Sick!

I DID IT! ✔

TURN OVER FOR MORE!

8

GO TO AN FA CUP FINAL!

THE WALK UP Wembley Way, singing along to *Abide With Me*, lapping up the amazing cup final atmosphere and being able to tell your mates on Monday morning you were there – YOU were at the FA Cup final. Priceless!

I DID IT! ✓

WHAT THE BIG DAY COSTS...

- Train ticket to London £20
- Tube ticket to Wembley Park £6.60
- FA Cup final ticket £45
- Match-day programme £10
- Half-time fish and chips £8.70
- The memory of being at the FA Cup final **Priceless**

EAT YOURSELF SILLY IN MORECAMBE!

9

SEEMS A BIT random, but if you want to sample the best pies in footy – and, come on, if you go to the football you've GOT to have a pie – then you need to head to the Globe Arena, home of Morecambe. Tasty!

 I DID IT! ✓

GLOBE ARENA

MORECAMBE FC

PETER McGUIGAN STAND

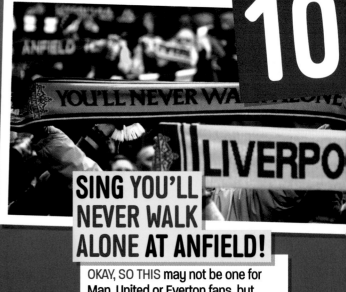

10

SING YOU'LL NEVER WALK ALONE AT ANFIELD!

OKAY, SO THIS may not be one for Man. United or Everton fans, but very few things get the goosebumps standing to attention like a full-on rendition of the famous Liverpool anthem. If you can get there for a big UCL night, too, even better!

I DID IT! ✓

11 TRAVEL TO AN AWAY GAME!

THERE'S SOMETHING a bit more special about following your team away from home – whether it's in the car with your scarf fluttering out of the window, on the train counting down the stops or on the supporters' coach stopping off at the services. However, that journey home can be a long, depressing one if your team have lost!

I DID IT! ✔

12 GO TO A CHAMPIONS LEAGUE KNOCKOUT MATCH!

ONCE THAT UNMISTAKABLE operatic music starts and the UCL centre circle flag starts rippling, you know you're attending something special. The Champions League is the world's top club footy competition and you've got to taste it at some point!

I DID IT! ✔

13 SCORE YOUR ULTIMATE WONDERGOAL!

MY ULTIMATE WONDERGOAL IS...
- ✔ Overhead kick
- ✔ Thumping volley
- ✔ Diving header
- ✔ Curling free-kick
- ✔ Long-range blaster
- ✔ Other

WHEN IT COMES to Pot Noodles, we've all got our own favourites – and it's the same with wondergoals. Some of us like rasping volleys that rattle in off the underside of the bar, others prefer acrobatic bicycle kicks. So, decide what yours is and then pull it off in a match – preferably a cup final!

I DID IT! ✔

14 WATCH A MATCH IN EVERY DIVISION IN ENGLAND!

THERE'S LIFE outside the Premier League, you know. It might not be as shiny or as fragrant as the top flight but the Football League, from Accrington to Wycombe, oozes tradition and every ground gives you a different experience!

I DID IT! ✔

TURN OVER FOR MORE! ▶

15

GO ON A TOUR OF THE BERNABEU!

YOU MIGHT not bump into this man but you will see a LOT of trophies – including a record-breaking 12 Champions League titles – as you stroll around the iconic home of Europe's most successful club, Real Madrid!

I DID IT! ✔

16

WATCH A MATCH AT A WEIRD STADIUM!

THE BERNABEU may be one of the world's most famous stadiums but it doesn't tick the weird and wonderful box – unlike Braga's epic cliff-face home in Portugal or Gibraltar's Victoria Stadium in the shadow of the Rock. The world is littered with quirky stadiums – see if you can find them!

I DID IT! ✔

17

READ ALL OF THESE BOOKS!

I DID IT! ✔

FOOTBALL ACADEMY SERIES
Tom Palmer
Experience the ups and downs of life as a Premier League academy player through the eyes of United FC Under-12s!

JAMIE JOHNSON COLLECTION
Dan Freedman
Follow the adventures of 11-year-old Jamie Johnson – a boy with a dream and a boy who lives and breathes football!

FOOTBALL SCHOOL – WHERE FOOTBALL EXPLAINS THE WORLD
Alex Bellos & Ben Lyttleton
Learn about the world through the eyes of footy – it's packed with true stories, science and facts!

THE FOOTBALL BOY WONDER – THE CHARLIE FRY SERIES
Martin Smith
Charlie Fry dreams of becoming a star – one day something happens that changes his life forever!

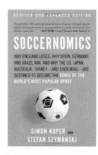

SOCCERNOMICS
Simon Kuper & Stefan Szymanski
Forget what you know about football – this book delves into the stats and facts of the game to answer all the big questions!

INVERTING THE PYRAMID
Jonathan Wilson
A glorious guide to tactics, charting the history and evolution of the game from the 1800s to today. Not for young footy fans!

18

WIN A TROPHY!

MOVE THE piggy bank to make a trophy-shaped space on your shelf because there WILL be a cup there before long. It doesn't matter what it is – a league title, a cup triumph, a Player of the Year award or Most Improved Player gong, put 100% in on the training pitch and you WILL be rewarded!

I DID IT! ✓

19

BE A MASCOT (NOT A FURRY ONE!)

LET'S BE HONEST, most of us do NOT make it as a professional footballer. The idea of leading our team out as the skipper is a distant dream – so why not do it as a mascot instead? You get to meet all of your heroes, have a kickabout on your team's pitch and get loads of wicked memories. Awesome!

I DID IT! ✓

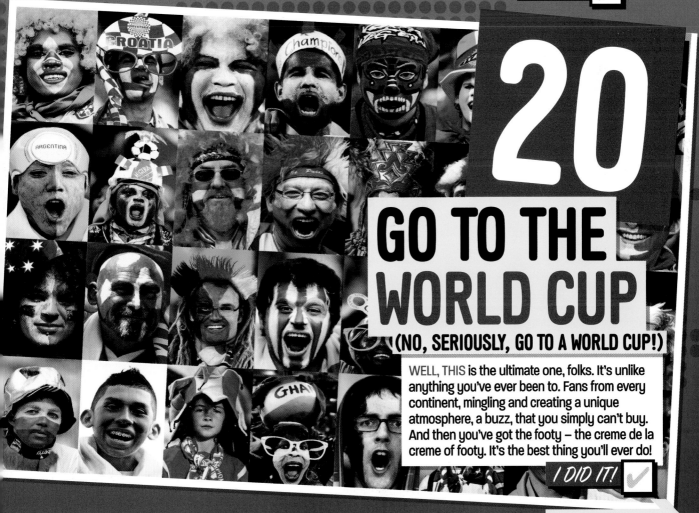

20

GO TO THE WORLD CUP
(NO, SERIOUSLY, GO TO A WORLD CUP!)

WELL, THIS is the ultimate one, folks. It's unlike anything you've ever been to. Fans from every continent, mingling and creating a unique atmosphere, a buzz, that you simply can't buy. And then you've got the footy – the creme de la creme of footy. It's the best thing you'll ever do!

I DID IT! ✓

TURN OVER FOR MORE! ➤

NOW WRITE IN YOUR OWN
BUCKET LIST IDEAS!

I DID IT!

1 .... ✓

2 .... ✓

3 .... ✓

4 .... ✓

5 .... ✓

6 .... ✓

7 .... ✓

8 .... ✓

9 .... ✓

10 .... ✓

PAZ'S FOOTY BUCKET LIST!

1 Watch Shrewsbury in the Premier League!
2 Go to a World Cup final...
3 ...and watch England win it!
4 Travel round South America watching footy!
5 Go for a burger with Romario!
6 Play five-a-side with Neymar!
7 Own a Sampdoria 1989 shirt!
8 Finish a World Cup sticker album!
9 Write a football-based sitcom!
10 Win the lottery and buy Shrewsbury!

How many have you done, dudes?

KETCH'S FOOTY BUCKET LIST!

1 See Newcastle lift ANYTHING silver and shiny!
2 Interview a Ballon d'Or winner!
3 Watch a World Cup final in the stadium!
4 Unveil a Rafa Benitez statue at St James' Park!
5 Stand on Borussia Dortmund's Yellow Wall!
6 Own a pair of Gigi Buffon match-worn gloves!
7 Walk on the pitch at Wembley!
8 Own Newcastle United Football Club!
9 Present Match of the Day!
10 Thumb-wrestle Alan Shearer!

My list is way better than yours, Paz!

ROBERTO FIRMINO

Liverpool

EMOJI FC

Imagine if the emojis formed a five-a-side team – it'd look a little bit like this...

FUNNY FREDDY

Emoji name: Crying with laughter

PROFILE: Meet the team joker, also known as bantersaurus rex and the king of the one-liners. Freddy fancies himself as a stand-up comedian and spends 99% of the day chuckling at his own gags!

POSITION: Keeper
PLAYING STYLE: The pitch is a stage – and the people deserve to be entertained. His motto is: don't do things simply if you can do it spectacularly! That goes for shot-stopping, cross-claiming and dealing with backpasses!
NICKNAMES: Lolzinho, Joke Book, Archbishop of Banterbury
FAVE ANIMAL: "I love chimpanzees!"
FOOTBALL HERO: Rene Higuita (Google him!)
MOST LIKELY TO SAY: "Ha-ha, ha-ha! That one always cracks me up!"
LEAST LIKELY TO SAY: "Can we just be serious for a second, lads?"

WACKY WAYNE

Emoji name: Crazy face

PROFILE: If Funny Freddy is the man with the gags, then this clown is his practical-joking, prankster, partner in crime. He's a lunatic who has no boundaries – he will do anything for a laugh... even if it involves actual pain!

POSITION: Defender
PLAYING STYLE: A manager's nightmare. He's unpredictable, he takes chances and he's prone to moments of absolute madness – this defensive goon gives his team-mates a heart-attack every time he's on the ball!
NICKNAMES: Wayne Loony, Idiot Chops, The Clown
FAVE ANIMAL: "A big daft panda!"
FOOTBALL HERO: David Luiz
MOST LIKELY TO SAY: "Eh, lads, lads – look at me, look at me!"
LEAST LIKELY TO SAY: "Nah, that sounds a bit dangerous to me!"

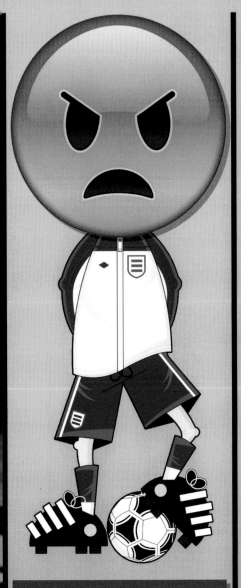

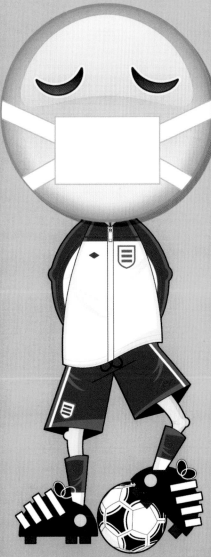

HOT-HEAD HARRY

Emoji name: Angry face

PROFILE: Angrier than a wounded wasp, this nutter could start an argument in a cardboard box. Everything gets him riled – you, me, soggy chips, lazy wingers, fussy refs... everything. You've been warned!

POSITION: Midfielder
PLAYING STYLE: Hot-headed and hard as nails, this thug would two-foot his gran if she had the ball. He loves a crunching tackle, shouting at team-mates and his mission is to destroy anything that moves!
NICKNAMES: Mr Grumble, The Mentalist, Psycho
FAVE ANIMAL: "Great white shark or scorpion!"
FOOTBALL HERO: Pepe
MOST LIKELY TO SAY: "Oi, you – you want some, yeah?!"
LEAST LIKELY TO SAY: "Sorry, that was my fault!"

SICKNOTE STEVE

Emoji name: Medical mask

PROFILE: This guy has more injuries and illnesses than an episode of *Casualty*. Every week it's something new – runny nose, itchy eye, pulled muscle – and he spends all day frantically Googling his symptoms!

POSITION: Winger
PLAYING STYLE: No-one knows – because no-one's ever seen him play a full 90 minutes. He spends more time on the treatment table than on the pitch, he's got the stamina of a sloth and is the king of shirk!
NICKNAMES: Illington, Sergeant Sniffles, Glass Man
FAVE ANIMAL: "My mum's pet goldfish!"
FOOTBALL HERO: Jack Wilshere
MOST LIKELY TO SAY: "I think I'm coming down with something!"
LEAST LIKELY TO SAY: "It's just a knock – I can run it off!"

COOL CONNOR

Emoji name: Smiling with shades

PROFILE: The coolest kid in town – strutting around like he owns the place, oozing charisma and charm. He's got the latest gadgets, the sickest gear and totally loves taking a cheeky selfie or two!

POSITION: Striker
PLAYING STYLE: This guy is a match-winner – one chance, one goal. Cool Connor is clinical, lethal – and very, very selfish. He's on free-kicks and penalties and, according to him, it's a one-man team!
NICKNAMES: Ice-man, Sir Hog-the-ball, Conaldo
FAVE ANIMAL: "Gotta be a lion!"
FOOTBALL HERO: Cristiano Ronaldo
MOST LIKELY TO SAY: "Just call me the postman – because I always deliver!"
LEAST LIKELY TO SAY: "To me, football is a team game!"

Let's do this!

EURO GIANTS CROSSWORD!

Get your footy brain in gear for some tricky teasers!

HOW DID YOU DO? TURN TO p92 FOR THE ANSWERS!

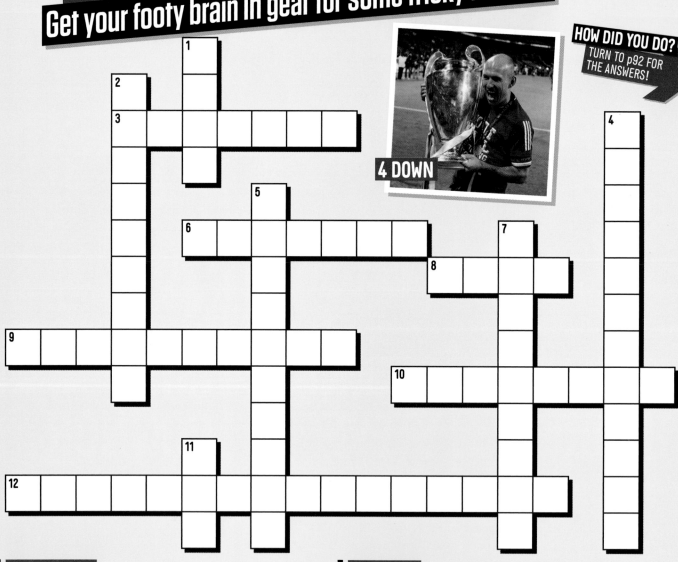

4 DOWN

ACROSS
3 Italian giants known as The Rossoneri (1, 1, 5)
6 Portuguese club which plays at the Estadio Da Luz (7)
8 33-time Dutch champions from Amsterdam (4)
9 Iconic club of Ferenc Puskas, Alfredo Di Stefano and Gareth Bale (4, 6)
10 Most successful Italian club of all time (8)
12 The BVB managed by Peter Bosz (8, 8)

DOWN
1 Team from the Italian capital (4)
2 The 1993 UCL winners (9)
4 Seven-time UCL winners from the Bavarian region of Germany (6, 6)
5 Italians sponsored by Pirelli since 1995 (5, 5)
7 Mes que un club (9)
11 French club owned by Oryx Qatar Sports Investments (1, 1, 1)

ROBERT LEWANDOWSKI

Bayern Munich

Kylian Mbappe

by Shedcreative (Josh French)

AGE 28 SUPPORTS MILLWALL
FAVE PLAYER TIM CAHILL
ART KYLIAN MBAPPE, PSG
DURATION FOUR TO FIVE HOURS

SHEDCREATIVE SAYS:
"Everyone loves a wonderkid!
His performances in the
Champions League against
Man. City and Dortmund
last season inspired
me to illustrate him!"

I LOVE ART
BECAUSE....
"It's very fun and you
can create something
unique and original!"

shedcreativedesign.com

TOP TIP
"Be brave, be
inspired – and
enjoy it!"

THE BEST ART GALLERY IN THE WORLD!

Get to know some of the sickest footy illustrators on the planet!

TURN OVER NOW!

2

1

3

ROOM 1

1 Paul Pogba
by Dave Merrell

AGE **40** SUPPORTS **MAN. CITY**
FAVE PLAYER **GABRIEL JESUS**
ART **PAUL POGBA, FRANCE**
DURATION **THREE DAYS**

DAVE SAYS: "Pog is an exciting young footballer, so I did this piece for a special exhibition!"

I LOVE ART BECAUSE...
"It allows me to express my passion for football!"

TOP ART TIP
"Don't be afraid to try new things and NEVER give up!"

davemerrell.com

2 Ace17
by Dan Leydon

AGE **30** SUPPORTS **LIVERPOOL**
FAVE PLAYER **DIRK KUYT**
ART **ADIDAS ACE 17 BOOTS**
DURATION **TWO HOURS**

DAN SAYS: "I wanted to show that no matter the price, all boots end up the same way!"

I LOVE ART BECAUSE...
"You get to speak to people all over the world about it!"

TOP ART TIP
"Draw every day and finish everything!"

danleydon.com

3 Marco Reus
by Dave Will

AGE **33** SUPPORTS **LIVERPOOL**
FAVE PLAYER **LUIS SUAREZ**
ART **MARCO REUS, B. DORTMUND**
DURATION **ONE HOUR**

DAVE SAYS: "Reus is an exciting player, so I tried him in this Subbuteo style!"

I LOVE ART BECAUSE...
"This is a mix of the two things I have a passion for!"

TOP ART TIP
"Never stop practising new techniques!"

davewilldesign.com

KING HARRY

4

5

6

I'M FOREVER BLOWING BUBBLES
PRETTY BUBBLE IN THE AIR

7

4 Harry Kane

by Elliott Sharp Designs

AGE 19 SUPPORTS MAN. UNITED
FAVE PLAYER PAUL POGBA
ART HARRY KANE, TOTTENHAM
DURATION FOUR TO FIVE HOURS

ELLIOT SAYS: "He proved doubters wrong again for a third season running. What a player!"

I LOVE ART BECAUSE... "It's great to see people enjoy work you've spent time on!"

TOP ART TIP "Be inspired by others and find styles you like!"

@ellsharpdesigns

5 Mesut Ozil

by Dave Flanagan

AGE 40 SUPPORTS MAN. CITY
FAVE PLAYER ANDREA PIRLO
ART MESUT OZIL, ARSENAL
DURATION THREE HOURS

DAVE SAYS: "I drew this for Arsenal to celebrate Mesut's birthday. He's an assist machine!"

I LOVE ART BECAUSE... "It's my favourite thing. I've done this since I was little!"

TOP ART TIP "Experiment with your work and get it out there!"

daveflanagan.co.uk

6 Marcus Rashford

by John Sheehan

AGE 27 SUPPORTS MAN. UNITED
FAVE PLAYER DAVID BECKHAM
ART MARCUS RASHFORD, MAN. UNITED
DURATION FOUR HOURS

JOHN SAYS: "Rashford is great. This is part of a big social-media project I put together!"

I LOVE ART BECAUSE... "It's the satisfaction you get when you finish a piece of work!"

TOP ART TIP "Get your work out there to raise your profile!"

john-sportraits.com

7 Michail Antonio

by Ethan Deery

AGE 14 SUPPORTS LIVERPOOL
FAVE PLAYER SADIO MANE
ART MICHAIL ANTONIO, WEST HAM
DURATION TWO HOURS

ETHAN SAYS: "Antonio put in some great performances, so I wanted to show him support!"

I LOVE ART BECAUSE... "It combines my two favourite things – football and art!"

TOP ART TIP "Cover loads of teams and players to get noticed!"

@ED_Illustration

TURN OVER FOR MORE!

8

9

11

10

ROOM 2

8 Ronaldinho

by Scott McRoy

AGE 30 SUPPORTS LIVERPOOL
FAVE PLAYER SADIO MANE
ART RONALDINHO, BARCELONA
DURATION TWO DAYS

SCOTT SAYS: "Ronaldinho is a footy legend and the colours represent his flamboyant playing style!"

I LOVE ART BECAUSE…
"You have freedom to create whatever you like. Plus, it's cool!"

TOP ART TIP
"Reach out to artists for advice like I once did!"

scottmcroy.com

9 Mohamed Salah

by Dave Vandepeer

AGE 47 SUPPORTS LIVERPOOL
FAVE PLAYER PHILIPPE COUTINHO
ART MOHAMED SALAH, LIVERPOOL
DURATION THREE HOURS

DAVE SAYS: "I was buzzing when he signed for Liverpool. He's got pace and is an exciting player!"

I LOVE ART BECAUSE…
"I love football and getting the likeness of a player gives me a buzz!"

TOP ART TIP
"Share it online. You never know who'll see it!"

footballcartoon.co.uk

10 Paulo Dybala

by Matthew Shipley

AGE 28 SUPPORTS BARCELONA
FAVE PLAYER LIONEL MESSI
ART PAULO DYBALA, JUVENTUS
DURATION TWO TO FOUR HOURS

MATTHEW SAYS: "I draw a range of footballers and Paulo was next on my hitlist. He's a great striker!"

I LOVE ART BECAUSE…
"I just love to draw – especially footballers!"

TOP ART TIP
"Learn the basics and you'll be able to draw anything!"

shipleyillustration.com

DAVID
DE GEA
MANCHESTER UNITED FC

12

13

14

11 Cristiano Ronaldo

by Mathew Vieira

AGE 28 SUPPORTS ARSENAL
FAVE PLAYER CRISTIANO RONALDO
ART CRISTIANO RONALDO, PORTUGAL
DURATION TEN HOURS

MATHEW SAYS: "I come from the same town as Ronaldo. He was incredible at Euro 2016!"

I LOVE ART BECAUSE... "You get a real buzz seeing the finished product!"

TOP ART TIP "Set goals for yourself. Hard work pays off!"

mathewvieira.com

12 David De Gea

by Hannah Carroll Design

AGE 22 SUPPORTS MAN. UNITED
FAVE PLAYER HENRIKH MKHITARYAN
ART DAVID DE GEA, MAN. UNITED
DURATION EIGHT HOURS

HANNAH SAYS: "De Gea is one of the best keepers in the world. He has a real presence in goal!"

I LOVE ART BECAUSE... "There's no right or wrong. You can be as creative as you like!"

TOP ART TIP "Test out different techniques to find what suits you!"

behance.net/hannahcarrolldesign

13 Sadio Mane

by Phil Galloway

AGE 36 SUPPORTS LIVERPOOL
FAVE PLAYER XABI ALONSO
ART SADIO MANE, LIVERPOOL
DURATION FOUR TO FIVE HOURS

PHIL SAYS: "I thought Mane's flamboyant style was perfect for this graffiti-style effect!"

I LOVE ART BECAUSE... "I'm a football fan with a passion for art. What's not to love?"

TOP ART TIP "Develop your own style and have fun doing it!"

philgallowaydraws.co.uk

14 Lionel Messi

by Mark Johnson Design

AGE 29 SUPPORTS MAN. UNITED
FAVE PLAYER RONALDINHO
ART LIONEL MESSI, BARCELONA
DURATION 12 HOURS

MARK SAYS: "Leo's special talent entertains people week in, week out. The world's best!"

I LOVE ART BECAUSE... "It's a way to express yourself using different styles!"

TOP ART TIP "Keep practising. Hard work pays off in the end!"

markjohnsondesign.co.uk

WHO'S THE OLDEST?

Two players, one simple question – tick the oldest...

HOW DID YOU DO? TURN TO p92 FOR THE ANSWERS!

1

LIONEL MESSI *OR* LUIS SUAREZ

2

JAMES MILNER *OR* LAURENT KOSCIELNY

3

KARIM BENZEMA *OR* GONZALO HIGUAIN

4

ANDER HERRERA *OR* MORGAN SCHNEIDERLIN

5

JAMIE VARDY *OR* DIEGO COSTA

6

CHRISTIAN BENTEKE *OR* DANIEL STURRIDGE

7

HUGO LLORIS *OR* TOM HEATON

8

ALEXIS SANCHEZ *OR* MESUT OZIL

9

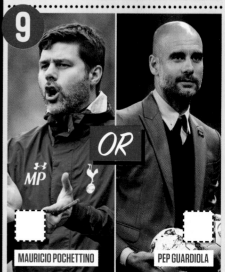

MAURICIO POCHETTINO *OR* PEP GUARDIOLA

For more quiz action check out bbc.co.uk/cbbc/games

ANTOINE GRIEZMANN

Atletico Madrid

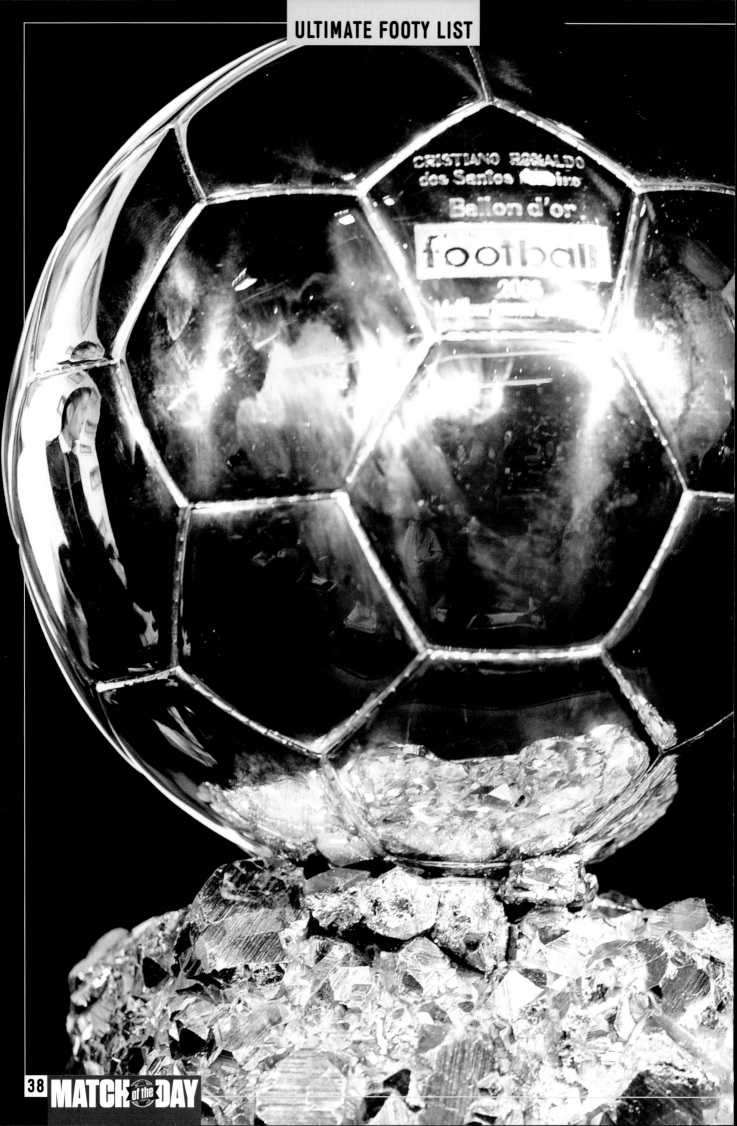

CRISTIANO RONALDO
dos Santos Aveiro
Ballon d'or
football
2008

WORLD PLAYER OF THE YEAR

...for the next TEN years!

Cristiano Ronaldo is nailed on to pick up another Ballon d'Or in January – but who will be celebrating over the next decade?

IT'S TIME
TO STEP
INTO THE
FUTURE!

TURN OVER NOW!

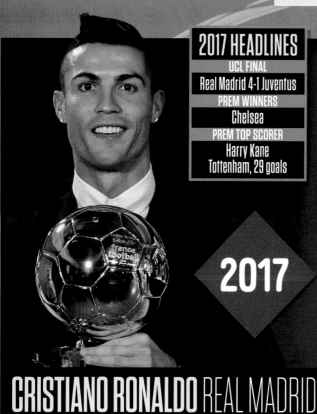

2017 HEADLINES

UCL FINAL
Real Madrid 4-1 Juventus

PREM WINNERS
Chelsea

PREM TOP SCORER
Harry Kane
Tottenham, 29 goals

2017

CRISTIANO RONALDO REAL MADRID

A FIFTH BALLON d'Or for Cristiano – all thanks to an epic end to the season. He bags a phenomenal 16 goals in his last ten games to pretty much single-handedly win the Spanish title AND the Champions League. Textbook Ronaldo – scoring big goals on the biggest stage!

2018

2018 HEADLINES

UCL FINAL
Bayern Munich 2-1 Man. City

PREM WINNERS
Man. City

PREM TOP SCORER
Harry Kane
Tottenham, 27 goals

2019 HEADLINES

UCL FINAL
Bayern Munich 5-0 Liverpool

PREM WINNERS
Tottenham

PREM TOP SCORER
Harry Kane
Man. United, 33 goals

2019

HARRY KANE TOTTENHAM

KANE'S STUNNING HAT-TRICK against Brazil in the World Cup final not only seals England's first tournament win since 1966, it also sees him become the first English Ballon d'Or winner since 2001. Kane's 12 goals in Russia also win him the Golden Boot – and a £250m move to Man. United!

PHIL JONES BAYERN MUNICH

EYEBROWS ARE RAISED when German giants Bayern Munich sign Phil Jones – even more so when they hand him the No.9 shirt and captain's armband. But Jones repays the faith shown in him by scoring 68 goals – breaking a 46-year-old club record for goals scored in one season!

2020

2020 HEADLINES
UCL FINAL
AC Milan 3-2 Man. United
PREM WINNERS
Man. United
PREM TOP SCORER
Harry Kane
Man. United, 37 goals

OLIVIER GIROUD AC MILAN

SHOCKED-FACE EMOJIS all round as Olivier Giroud bags the award after a sick debut season at the San Siro. The 34-year-old French striker, written off by experts after his £100 million move to Italy, caps off a stunning season by scoring the winner in the Euro 2020 final!

2021

2021 HEADLINES
UCL FINAL
Real Madrid 1-0 Juventus
PREM WINNERS
Man. City
PREM TOP SCORER
Ousmane Dembele
Man. City, 28 goals

LEIGH GRIFFITHS REAL MADRID

FOLLOWING C-RON'S DECISION to quit footy to become the president of Portugal, Real turn to 31-year-old Scotland striker Leigh Griffiths. The ex-Celtic forward scores 55 goals as Real claim a league and UCL double! Griffiths is also top scorer in World Cup qualifying. Craziness!

TURN OVER FOR MORE!

2022

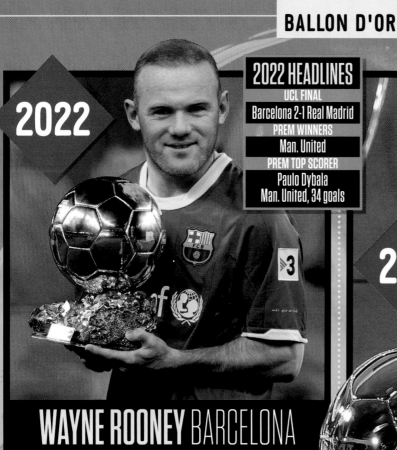

2024

WAYNE ROONEY BARCELONA

ENGLAND RETAIN the World Cup thanks to 37-year-old Wazza, who comes out of international retirement to play in the tournament. His goals v Germany in the final cap off an epic year, which sees him released by Everton, sign for Barca, win the UCL and duet with Katy Perry for the Xmas No.1!

2023

ZLATAN IBRAHIMOVIC MALMO

NEYMAR REAL MADRID

SWEDISH MINNOWS MALMO produce the greatest shock of all time in the UCL final – and it's all down to legendary striker Zlatan. The ex-Man. United man, now 41, who quit football in 2018 to live in an igloo in the north of Sweden, rejoins his old club and scores four in the final. Unreal!

NINE MONTHS AFTER his controversial £300m move back to Spain from PSG causes riots in Barcelona, Neymar secures the La Liga title with a hat-trick in the last game of the season against his old club Barca. He repeats the feat in the UCL final – including a cheeky late winner!

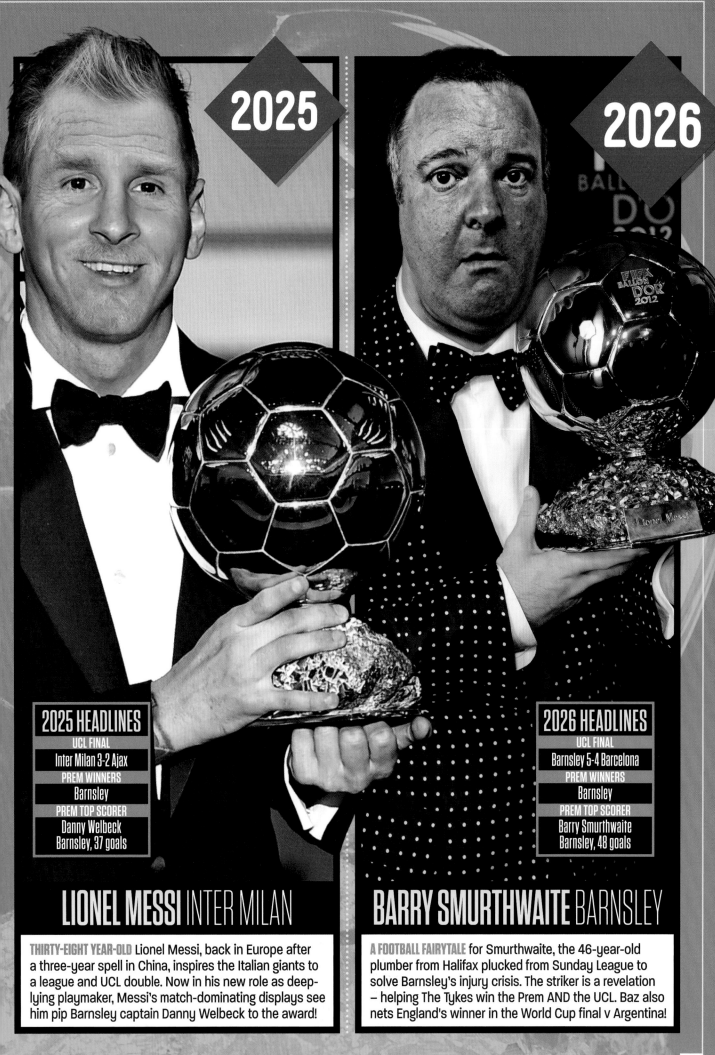

2025

2025 HEADLINES

UCL FINAL
Inter Milan 3-2 Ajax

PREM WINNERS
Barnsley

PREM TOP SCORER
Danny Welbeck
Barnsley, 37 goals

LIONEL MESSI INTER MILAN

THIRTY-EIGHT YEAR-OLD Lionel Messi, back in Europe after a three-year spell in China, inspires the Italian giants to a league and UCL double. Now in his new role as deep-lying playmaker, Messi's match-dominating displays see him pip Barnsley captain Danny Welbeck to the award!

2026

2026 HEADLINES

UCL FINAL
Barnsley 5-4 Barcelona

PREM WINNERS
Barnsley

PREM TOP SCORER
Barry Smurthwaite
Barnsley, 48 goals

BARRY SMURTHWAITE BARNSLEY

A FOOTBALL FAIRYTALE for Smurthwaite, the 46-year-old plumber from Halifax plucked from Sunday League to solve Barnsley's injury crisis. The striker is a revelation – helping The Tykes win the Prem AND the UCL. Baz also nets England's winner in the World Cup final v Argentina!

THE COUNTRY QUIZ!

Just tell us which nation the clubs below come from...

HOW DID YOU DO? TURN TO p92 FOR THE ANSWERS!

1

- A Germany
- B Austria
- C Switzerland

2

- A Serbia
- B Croatia
- C Hungary

3

- A Germany
- B Belgium
- C Czech Republic

4

- A Holland
- B Belgium
- C Russia

5

- A Chile
- B Bolivia
- C Botswana

6

- A Brazil
- B Argentina
- C Portugal

7
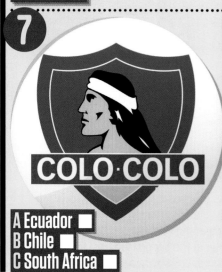
- A Ecuador
- B Chile
- C South Africa

8
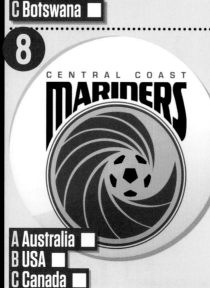
- A Australia
- B USA
- C Canada

9

- A France
- B Slovakia
- C Austria

MESUT ÖZIL

Arsenal

Just imagine the perfect week of television – it'd look something like this. Honk!

MONDAY

Cock-A-Doodle-Roo
BBC One 7am
Start the day with Everton star Wayne Rooney and his feathered friend Captain Chicken. This morning, Aston Villa manager Steve Bruce attempts the infamous Coco-Pop Challenge.

Bak To The Drawing Board
BBC One 11am
Chelsea midfielder Tiemoue Bakayoko is in a race against time to get his licence from the Architects Registration Board, as he plans to construct his dream home out of Kit-Kats.

Vagner Love Island
BBC One 10pm
Shipwrecked Brazilian striker Vagner Love washes up on a south pacific island, before being greeted by the most gruesome of sights. How on earth will the baller survive this horrific ordeal?

Devil's Advocaat
BBC Four 10.30pm
Join Holland manager Dick Advocaat for another session of his lively debates from University College London. This week, Dick claims that sheep are really clouds that have learnt how to baa.

TUESDAY

Rat Up A Drainpipe
BBC One 7pm
Romanian left-back Razvan Rat attempts to clamber up the drainpipe of St Paul's Cathedral with no safety harness. Will his decision to smoother himself in Vaseline prove foolish?

Motta v Otter
BBC Two 8.30pm
PSG midfielder Thiago Motta continues his hunt for the elusive giant otter in the Amazon rainforest armed only with Mini Babybels, a cattle prod and his trusty banjo. Last in series.

Knock, Knock, Who's There?
BBC Two 9pm
Fly-on-the-wall series following Brighton winger Anthony Knockaert as he prepares for his first ever stand-up comedy gig. This week, a visit to John Bishop's house ends in disaster for John's new carpet.

Naked Karate: Zarate v Abate
BBC One 10pm
Live coverage of the much-hyped first-round clash between Watford frontman Mauro Zarate and AC Milan full-back Ignazio Abate. Hosted by John Inverdale.

WEDNESDAY

Holmes Under The Hammer
BBC One 10.30am
Eamonn Holmes' attempt to give West Ham ace Angelo Ogbonna a piggy-back around the London Stadium ends with a trip to A&E.

Clyne In The Tyne
BBC One 7pm
Everyone's favourite escapologist Nathaniel Clyne is back in action – this week attempting to free himself from a padlocked suitcase tossed into the River Tyne.

Hip-Hop Klopp
BBC Two 9pm
Jurgen's got his swagger back and continues his quest to become a superstar rapper. His performance of Jay-Z's 2004 hit *99 Problems* earns him a standing ovation at Crosby Comrades Club.

Trump In Your Face
BBC News 11pm
US president Donald Trump returns for another series of his talk show. This week, Tony Pulis gets a grilling about the time he happy-slapped a llama at Chester Zoo.

THURSDAY

Mou Mou The Choo Choo
CBeebies 8am
Cartoon fun with everyone's fave steam train. The grouchy locomotive heads to Wales for a break – but a cliff-top disaster looms thanks to a clumsy seagull. D'oh.

Song, Bong and Fearless Frimpong
BBC Three 7pm
Rubin Kazan's Alex Song and Brighton's Gaetan Bong challenge ex-Arsenal man Emmanuel Frimpong to skate down the M6 blindfolded. Don't try this at home.

Bob's Your Uncle
BBC Two 8pm
Documentary following Fleetwood midfielder Bobby Grant as he attempts to track down his long lost nephew in the Australian outback. Bob's decision to tickle a sleeping koala sparks a brawl.

Pack It Up, Pack It In
BBC Four 11pm
On the 25th anniversary of House Of Pain's smash hit *Jump Around*, Bristol City midfielder Marlon Pack travels to Boston, USA, to chart the rise and fall of the mid-1990s rap band.

FRIDAY

Alex Oxlade-Chambermaid
BBC One 11am
The England star swaps life as a footballer for the Swiss ski resort of St Moritz, where he works as a housekeeper. But how will he react when an OAP steals his mop?

Mike Dean Disco Queen
BBC Four 8.30pm
Join the hot-steppin, body-poppin ref for another late night boogie. This week, the Prem whistler heads to Blackpool where he's joined by Andre Mariner and Martin Atkinson.

Rash, Bang, Wallop
BBC Two 9pm
Foam mallets at the ready as Marcus Rashford takes to the streets of Oldham to bash some unsuspecting pensioners. Contains strong language and violence.

Ings, Mings & The Chicken Wings
BBC One 10pm
Danny Ings and Tyrone Mings star as two blundering but lovable flatmates. Danny takes a delivery of 20 baby chickens after a mix up with the local Chinese takeaway.

SATURDAY

Harry The Haddock
CBBC 7am
Cartoon capers with Harry Maguire, the saltwater superhero. The ex-Leicester defender, turned into a fish after swallowing a magic maggot, must rescue Princess Prawn from the evil Colonel Crab.

Big Sam's Bouncy Castle Bedlam
BBC One 7pm
Sam Allardyce hosts another episode of his chaotic award-winning wibbly-wobbly gameshow, with Ronald Koeman and Vanessa Feltz.

Emre Can Or Emre Can't
BBC One 7.30pm
The Liverpool man tackles a series of challenges. Can he avoid the dreaded gunge tank this week?

Blind As A bat
BBC Two 8pm
Dutch defender Daley Blind travels around Manchester dressed as a Common Pipistrelle bat, handing out free scotch eggs and pork pies to the city's waifs and strays.

SUNDAY

Poch & Pooch
CBeebies 7am
Epic cartoon adventure starring cheeky scamp Mauricio Pochettino and his pet dog Pooch. This week, Poch is potty training Pooch – but it's not going to plan.

Ant's In His Pants
BBC Two 1pm
Man. United's Anthony Martial is back in his furry Y-fronts attempting, once again, to catch and lick a live, native British mammal. This week, he's after a feisty European badger.

Foster The Imposter
BBC Two 5.30pm
Award-winning hidden camera show. West Brom keeper Ben Foster is back up to his old tricks impersonating an escaped prisoner – much to the horror of six French exchange pupils!

All The Fun Of The Fair With Scott Sinclair
BBC Four 10pm
The Celtic man explores the history of the fairground – and discovers a chilling family secret about the ghost train.

2016-17 LEAGU

JUVENTUS
SERIE A CHAMPIONS

REAL MADRID
LA LIGA CHAMPIONS

BAYERN MUNICH
BUNDESLIGA CHAMPIONS

WINNERS!

CELTIC
SCOTTISH PREM CHAMPIONS

MONACO
LIGUE 1 CHAMPIONS

ALVARO MORATA

Chelsea

THE ULTIMATE GUIDE TO...
RUSSIA
2018
Check out the official logo!
It's got Brazil's name on it!
Dream on, Gab – we're winning this!
THE STARS, STADIUMS, STATS & SLANG!
TURN OVER NOW!

RUSSIA 2018

Russia is ready, and you will be too once you've read this guide to the biggest footy festival on the planet!

THE FACTS!

Capital: Moscow
Population: 144,463,451
Size: 6,323,482 miles sq
Currency: Ruble
President: Vladimir Putin

5 THINGS YOU NEED TO KNOW!

1 Everything kicks off on Thursday 14 June 2018!

2 This will be the 21st World Cup finals!

3 32 teams will battle it out across 32 days!

4 12 awesome stadiums in 11 Russian cities!

5 On Sunday 15 July 2018 one nation will lift the trophy!

MOSCOW!

Think ballet, history and crazy colourful buildings! The city's 81k capacity stadium will host the big final!

5 GOLDEN BOOT CONTENDERS!

Gabriel Jesus Brazil
Four years ago he was painting the streets green and yellow for Brazil 2014 – now he's their top striker!

Antoine Griezmann France
Approaching his peak and playing up top in a team of serious talent – a real contender!

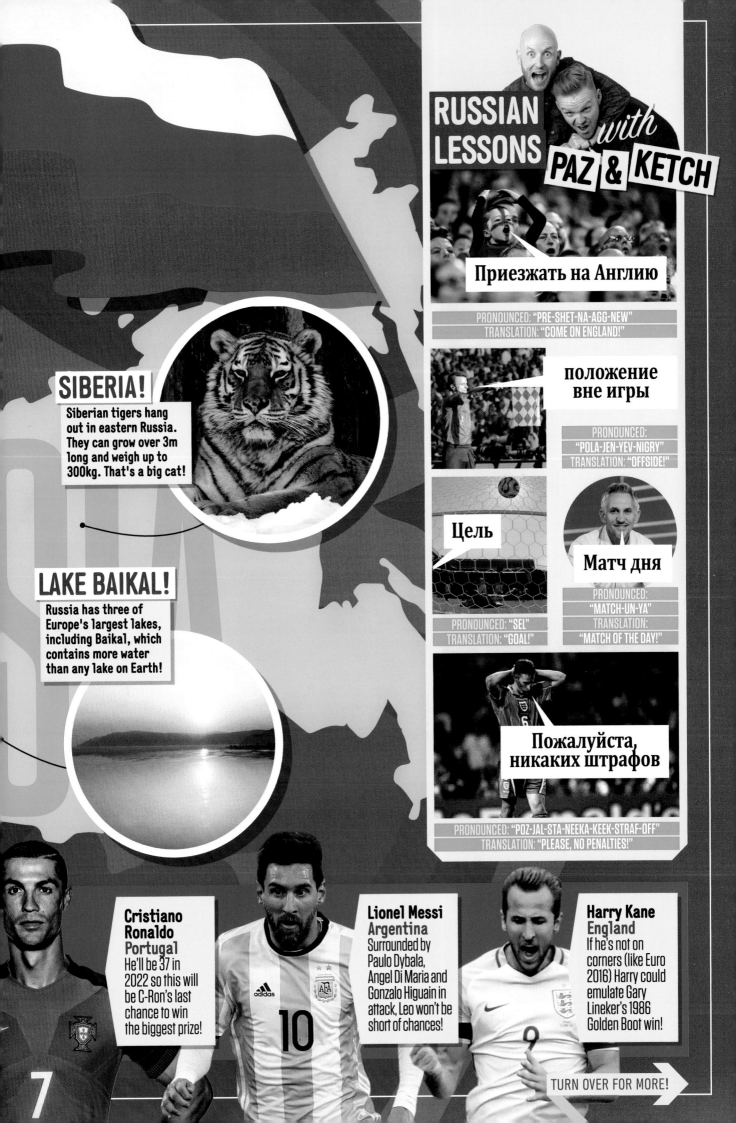

RUSSIAN LESSONS with PAZ & KETCH

Приезжать на Англию

PRONOUNCED: "PRE-SHET-NA-AGG-NEW"
TRANSLATION: "COME ON ENGLAND!"

положение вне игры

PRONOUNCED: "POLA-JEN-YEV-NIGRY"
TRANSLATION: "OFFSIDE!"

Цель

PRONOUNCED: "SEL"
TRANSLATION: "GOAL!"

Матч дня

PRONOUNCED: "MATCH-UN-YA"
TRANSLATION: "MATCH OF THE DAY!"

Пожалуйста, никаких штрафов

PRONOUNCED: "POZ-JAL-STA-NEEKA-KEEK-STRAF-OFF"
TRANSLATION: "PLEASE, NO PENALTIES!"

SIBERIA!

Siberian tigers hang out in eastern Russia. They can grow over 3m long and weigh up to 300kg. That's a big cat!

LAKE BAIKAL!

Russia has three of Europe's largest lakes, including Baikal, which contains more water than any lake on Earth!

Cristiano Ronaldo
Portugal
He'll be 37 in 2022 so this will be C-Ron's last chance to win the biggest prize!

Lionel Messi
Argentina
Surrounded by Paulo Dybala, Angel Di Maria and Gonzalo Higuain in attack, Leo won't be short of chances!

Harry Kane
England
If he's not on corners (like Euro 2016) Harry could emulate Gary Lineker's 1986 Golden Boot win!

7

TURN OVER FOR MORE!

WHO'S GONNA WIN IT?

We reckon it's gonna be one of these amazing nations!

THE REIGNING CHAMPS!

BEST WORLD CUP RESULTS: Winners (1954, 1974, 1990, 2014)

GERMANY

STAR MEN

MANUEL NEUER

JULIAN DRAXLER

MESUT OZIL

THE CURRENT WORLD champs have reached the semi-finals in their last seven major tournaments. In three of those they went on to make the final! They're cool, calm, collected and will be desperate to become back-to-back winners for the first time in 56 years!

FRANCE

THE SUPER SQUAD!

NO COUNTRY in the world can match the strength in depth of the French. Every position in the squad is loaded with top talent. Speed, strength, technique and experience. If they can get organised and find a style, this could be their tournament!

STAR MEN

PAUL POGBA

ANTOINE GRIEZMANN

N'GOLO KANTE

BRAZIL

NEYMAR'S SAMBA STARS!

THEY'VE WON this competition FIVE TIMES – more than any other country. They were the first nation to clinch qualification for this summer's tournament. And they have £198m PSG ace Neymar in their team – the world's most-expensive footballer. Beat that, dudes!

STAR MEN

NEYMAR

GABRIEL JESUS

THIAGO SILVA

SPAIN

THE POINT PROVERS!

DESPITE BEING TOURNAMENT favourites in Brazil four years ago, Spain failed to even get out of their group. They've waited a long time to rewrite that wrong and will head to Russia with largely the same squad of players – so they'll be hungry for success!

STAR MEN

SERGIO RAMOS

ANDRES INIESTA

DAVID SILVA

ENGLAND

THE OUTSIDERS!

THEY COULDN'T, COULD they? If England can summon the skill and spirit shown by the Under-20 squad, who won the World Cup for their age group last summer, maybe, just MAYBE, they could pull off a big, beautiful shock. Okay, we said maybe!

STAR MEN

HARRY KANE

DELE ALLI

ADAM LALLANA

THE AVERAGE WORLD CUP!

15 Senegal average 15 cards per World Cup – the highest average!

Average goals per World Cup:

MESSI 1.66

RONALDO 1

The highest ever average tournament attendance was 68,991 during USA 1994. Wow!

41,852 Average World Cup game attendance!

The biggest goal average was **5.4 goals** per game during the 1954 World Cup in Switzerland!

KEVIN DE BRUYNE

Man. City

LUKA MODRIC

Real Madrid

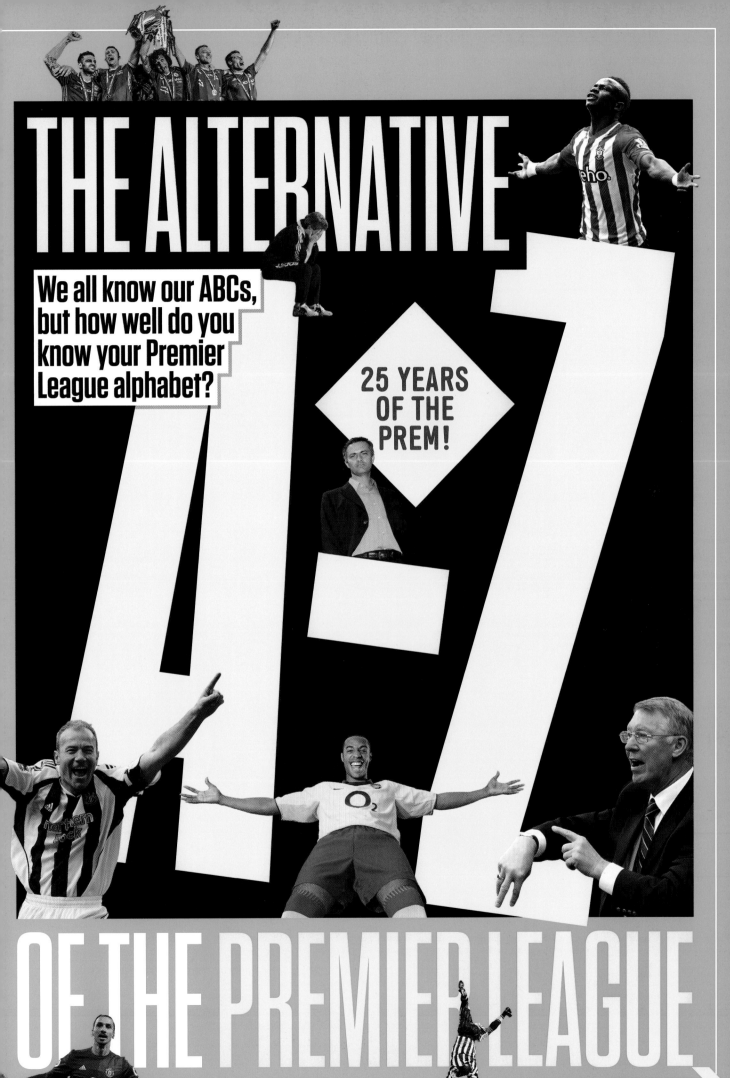

THE ALTERNATIVE A-Z OF THE PREMIER LEAGUE

We all know our ABCs, but how well do you know your Premier League alphabet?

25 YEARS OF THE PREM!

TURN OVER NOW!

A IS FOR ARSENAL

THE GUNNERS are one of six clubs who've played in all 25 Premier League seasons – can you name the other five? Clue – Man. City are not in this super six...

KETCH SAYS
Look at the state of that Arsenal away kit from the early 1990s – yuck!

ANSWER: Man. United, Liverpool, Chelsea, Everton, Tottenham

B IS FOR BRIAN DEANE

THE PREMIER LEAGUE was born at 3pm on Saturday 15 August 1992. Five minutes later Sheffield United striker Brian Deane (ask your dad) rose above the Man. United defence to score the first EVER goal in this famous division – history made!

C IS FOR CRAZY GANG

A NICKNAME given to the craziest bunch of footballers the Prem has ever seen. When Wimbledon's ragtag bunch of players weren't roughing up opponents in the 1990s they'd be playing practical jokes. No-one was safe – not even chairman Sam Hammam, widely considered the craziest of the lot!

D IS FOR DILLY DING, DILLY DONG

LEICESTER'S secret weapon during their world-famous Premier League title win was a little imaginary bell. Claudio Ranieri used this zany catchphrase to focus his players when their concentration dipped in training and during games – it worked. The Foxes won the title by ten points!

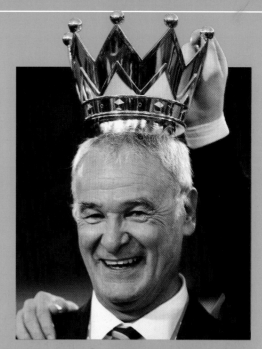

E IS FOR ENTERTAINERS

EASILY THE most exciting team to ever grace a Prem pitch. Kevin Keegan's 1995-96 Newcastle team had only two objectives – score more than the opposition and entertain everyone watching. They nearly always achieved these two things. But they also blew a 12-point lead in the title race. D'oh!

F IS FOR FERGIE TIME

WHEN Sir Alex Ferguson's Man. United teams hit stoppage time, needing an equaliser or winner, Fergie Time would be activated. All the fiery Scot had to do was scowl at the fourth official and point to his watch. If Fergie Time was not added on, referees risked facing The Hairdryer – see letter H!

PAZ SAYS
Fergie pointing to his watch was one of the scariest sights in footy. Aaargh!

TURN OVER FOR MORE!

G IS FOR GOAL-LINE TECH

THE PREM had been going for 21 years before goal-line technology arrived in 2013. Now 14 cameras are set up at every game to detect whether or not the whole ball crosses the line. We waited 21 years for it, so should have video refs by 2035. LOL!

H IS FOR HAIRDRYER

WAYNE ROONEY said there was "nothing worse" and it made Cristiano Ronaldo cry! When Alex Ferguson got mad he would shout in your face so loud it felt as though he was pointing a hairdryer directly at you on full power – not fun!

I IS FOR INVINCIBLES

THE GREATEST feat in Prem history? This was achieved by Arsene Wenger's 2003-04 Arsenal team, who went an entire season without losing a league game! They haven't won a title since!

PAZ SAYS
Thierry Henry bagged 228 Arsenal goals. Not bad, eh?!

J IS FOR JURGEN KLINSMANN

HE CAME, he scored, he dived! The German striker won over Tottenham fans in 1994 thanks to his knack for scoring and his epic diving celebration, which he invented after people accused him of going down too easily. Wunderbar!

K IS FOR KITS

MAN. UNITED **AWAY 1995-96**

CHELSEA **AWAY 1994-96**

ARSENAL **HOME 2005-06**

LEEDS **HOME 1995-96**

THE PREM has seen some good, bad and just plain ugly kits over the years! Here are a few standout threads...

NEWCASTLE **HOME & AWAY 1995-97**

L IS FOR LOVE IT

KETCH SAYS
Howay the lads!

AS THE 1995-96 season reached boiling point, Sir Alex Ferguson played his famous mind games on title rival Kevin Keegan. The crafty Red Devil said Nottingham Forest might not try as hard v Keegan's men as they had against his team. Keegan lost it live on TV – and The Toon lost to Forest three days later!

THE LOVE IT RANT IN FULL!

"I've kept really quiet but I'll tell you something, he went down in my estimation when he said that. We have not resorted to that. You can tell him now, we're still fighting for this title and he's got to go to Middlesbrough and get something – and I'll tell you, honestly, I will love it if we beat them – love it!"

TURN OVER FOR MORE!

M IS FOR MANE

TWO MINUTES 56 seconds. That's how long it took Sadio Mane to net a hat-trick for Southampton against Aston Villa in 2014-15 – the quickest in Prem history! He almost halved the previous record held for 21 years by Liverpool legend Robbie Fowler. His achievement may never be beaten!

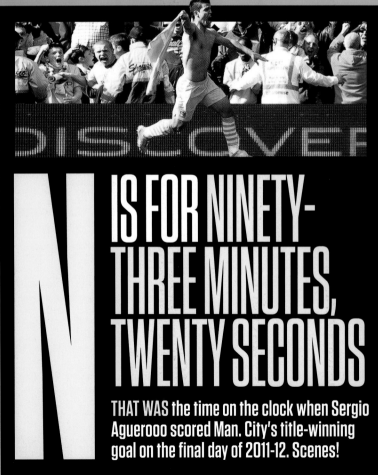

N IS FOR NINETY-THREE MINUTES, TWENTY SECONDS

THAT WAS the time on the clock when Sergio Aguerooo scored Man. City's title-winning goal on the final day of 2011-12. Scenes!

O IS FOR OWN GOALS

THE MOST unwanted record in Prem history belongs to ex-Everton, Man. City, Aston Villa and QPR centre-back Richard Dunne. He found the net TEN times in his top-flight career – his own net that is!

P IS FOR PIZZAGATE

WHEN Man. United won 2-0 v Arsenal at Old Trafford on 24 October 2004 the game was so heated a food fight broke out in the Old Trafford tunnel! Rumour has it Cesc Fabregas hurled a pizza slice at Fergie and he had to change clothes!

Q IS FOR QUICK

THE FASTEST speed ever clocked by a Prem player since records began belongs to Adama Traore. He hit 23mph at the Emirates Stadium for Middlesbrough in 2016. Don't let the cops see you doing those speeds, Ad!

R IS FOR ROMAN EMPIRE

WHEN RUSSIAN billionaire Roman Abramovich bought Chelsea in 2003, the Prem changed forever. In the 14 years since, Chelsea have won five titles. He's let 11 managers go (including Jose Mourinho twice!) and sunk over a billion pounds into the club. Wow!

PAZ SAYS
Lend us a fiver, Roman? LOL!

S IS FOR SPECIAL ONE

"PLEASE DON'T call me arrogant, but I'm European champion and I think I'm a special one!" This is how Jose Mourinho introduced himself to the Premier League when he took over at Chelsea in 2004 – and then he won it!

TURN OVER FOR MORE!

T

IS FOR TWO HUNDRED AND SIXTY GOALS

KETCH SAYS
Big Al is one of my all-time heroes – I've seen him score tons of goals at St James' Park!

THE RECORD number of Premier League goals hit by MOTD man Alan Shearer is an incredible 260. If Harry Kane can continue to find the net at the prolific rate he has for the last three seasons, he should hit 261 by 2025-26. Good luck, H!

U

IS FOR UNLUCKY 13

MAN. UNITED have won the Premier League title more than any other team – 13 times. Unlucky 13? United don't think so! Count them...

1992-93
1993-94
1995-96
1996-97
1998-99
1999-00
2000-01
2002-03
2006-07
2007-08
2008-09
2010-11
2012-13

V

IS FOR VAN GAAL'S DIVE

WE'VE WITNESSED some amazing touchline antics over the past 25 years but Louis van Gaal hurling himself to the floor in protest at Arsenal players diving against Man. United in 2016 may never be equalled. We're still laughing!

W IS FOR WORLD'S BEST

ROUND-THE-CLOCK news coverage, world-class clubs, huge transfer fees, insane competition, massive attendances and a superb average of 2.9 goals per game. This is what makes the Prem the best league in world footy. End of!

X IS FOR X-RATED

The Prem's had its share of X-rated moments – Eric Cantona's kung-fu kick, Roy Keane and Patrick Vieira's tunnel bust-up and Newcastle team-mates Lee Bowyer and Kieron Dyer fighting!

Y IS FOR ER, Y

A TOTAL of 15 teams have played in The Prem with Y in their name – can you name them all?

Z IS FOR ZLATAN

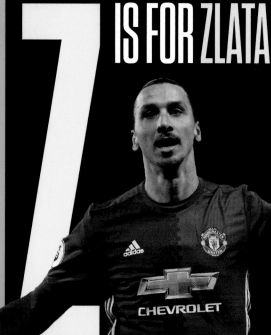

"I WON'T be the king of Manchester, I'll be the god of Manchester," said Zlatan Ibrahimovic ahead of his arrival in England. He got 17 goals in 28 games to seal his legend status!

Coventry City, Man City, Derby, Burnley, Bradford City, Swansea City, Hull City, Crystal Palace, Barnsley

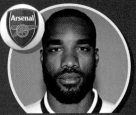

ALEXANDRE LACAZETTE

ARSENAL
£46.5m
From Lyon
July 2017

NATHAN AKE

BOURNEMOUTH
£20m
From Chelsea
June 2017

JOSE IZQUIERDO

BRIGHTON
£13.5m
From Club Brugge
August 2017

CHRIS WOOD

BURNLEY
£15m
From Leeds
August 2017

ALVARO MORATA

CHELSEA
£58m
From Real Madrid
July 2017

CHRISTIAN BENTEKE

CRYSTAL PALACE
£27m
From Liverpool
August 2016

GYLFI SIGURDSSON

EVERTON
£45m
From Swansea
August 2017

STEVE MOUNIE

HUDDERSFIELD
£11.5m
From Montpellier
July 2017

ISLAM SLIMANI

LEICESTER
£29m
From Sporting Lisbon
August 2016

NABY KEITA

LIVERPOOL
£55m
From RB Leipzig
August 2017

YOUR CLUB'S RECORD SIGNING!

The most expensive player in every Premier League club's history...

KEVIN DE BRUYNE

MAN. CITY
£55m
From Wolfsburg
August 2015

PAUL POGBA

MAN. UNITED
£89m
From Juventus
August 2016

MICHAEL OWEN

NEWCASTLE
£17m
From Real Madrid
August 2005

MARIO LEMINA

SOUTHAMPTON
£18m
From Juventus
August 2017

GIANNELLI IMBULA

STOKE
£18m
From Porto
February 2016

BORJA BASTON

SWANSEA
£15.5m
From Atletico Madrid
August 2016

DAVINSON SANCHEZ

TOTTENHAM
£42m
From Ajax
August 2017

ANDRE GRAY

WATFORD
£18.5m
From Burnley
August 2017

OLIVER BURKE

WEST BROM
£15m
From RB Leipzig
August 2017

MARKO ARNAUTOVIC

WEST HAM
£25m
From Stoke
July 2017

Check out the latest transfer rumours at bbc.co.uk/sport/football/gossip

PIERRE-EMERICK
AUBAMEYANG

Borussia Dortmund

FOOTBALL!

Six superstar vloggers tell us their football faves!

Q	TEKKERZ KID	SPENCER OWEN
Best player in the world?	"100% LEO MESSI!"	"Lionel Messi!"
Best team in the world?	"Mmm, Real Madrid!"	"Real Madrid!"
Fave player?	"Neymar – I love his skills and how he gets past defenders quickly!"	"Dan Brown from Hashtag United!"
2017–18 Premier League winners?	"I'm going to go for Spurs!"	"Man. United – with a proven Prem scorer in Lukaku they could go far!"
2018 World Cup winners?	"Germany are my pick!"	"Germany – they know how to win the big tournaments!"

JOHN FARNWORTH	KIERAN BROWN	CALFREEZY	STR SKILL SCHOOL

JOHN FARNWORTH

"N'Golo Kante!"

"Barcelona, of course!"

"Neymar!"

"I hope Man. United, but I think Chelsea will do it!"

"Germany, but I do have a soft spot for Brazil, too!"

KIERAN BROWN

"Cristiano Ronaldo!"

"Real Madrid!"

"Cristiano Ronaldo – again!"

"I think Liverpool can do it!"

"ENGLAND! Just kidding... I'll say Spain!"

CALFREEZY

"Ronaldo. The guy is a machine!"

"It's got to be Real Madrid. They're electric in attack!"

"Luis Suarez – I miss him at Liverpool!"

"I always say Liverpool, but Man. City have made some HUGE signings!"

"Germany are in good form and know how to win big tournaments!"

STR SKILL SCHOOL

"Messi is from another planet!"

"Barcelona can destroy any team!"

"Old school, but I'll say George Best!"

"Man. United – they have more power this season!"

"Mmm, maybe France, but I'll pick Germany!"

LUIS SUAREZ

Barcelona

A YEAR IN FOOTBALL!

How much can you remember about 2017? Let's find out...

HOW DID YOU DO? TURN TO p92 FOR THE ANSWERS!

1

Who finished as runners-up to Chelsea in the Prem last season?

A Man. City ☐
B Tottenham ☐
C Liverpool ☐

2

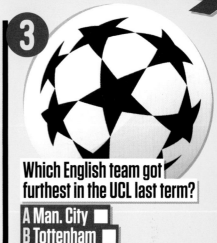

What was the score in the FA Cup final?

A Arsenal 1-0 Chelsea ☐
B Arsenal 2-1 Chelsea ☐
C Arsenal 3-1 Chelsea ☐

3

Which English team got furthest in the UCL last term?

A Man. City ☐
B Tottenham ☐
C Leicester ☐

4

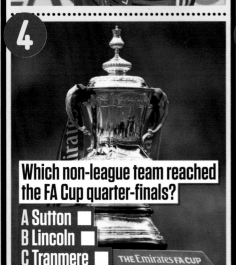

Which non-league team reached the FA Cup quarter-finals?

A Sutton ☐
B Lincoln ☐
C Tranmere ☐

5

Which team went 25 games unbeaten in the Prem in 2016-17?

A Chelsea ☐
B Tottenham ☐
C Man. United ☐

6

Who was top scorer in La Liga last season?

A Lionel Messi ☐
B Luis Suarez ☐
C Neymar ☐

7

Who scored the first goal in the 2017 UCL final?

A Mario Mandzukic ☐
B Cristiano Ronaldo ☐
C Casemiro ☐

8

Javier Hernandez joined West Ham from which club?

A Bayer Leverkusen ☐
B Wolfsburg ☐
C Eintracht Frankfurt ☐

9

Who did ex-England star Tony Adams boss for seven games?

A Malaga ☐
B Granada ☐
C Osasuna ☐

30 WAYS TO become a baller!

Want to be your team's tekkers don?
Then check out MOTD mag skills tips!

TURN OVER NOW!

1

Rock some sick wheels!

There's nothing quite like a fresh pair to give you that extra spark on the pitch. Look the part, feel the part, readers!

3

Train your weaknesses!

When Leo Messi was young his free-kicks were rank – so what did he do? He kept practising until he never missed one!

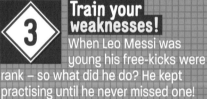

4

Celebrate like a boss!

Putting your hand in the air isn't enough! Be creative and come up with a sick celebration you can bust out every time you bag!

Get yourself a special move and stand out like Ozil!

2

Be confident!

Always believe in your own ability. If you don't get it right the first time, just try again. Trust your tekkers!

Study your hero!
5 Want to play like your favourite player? Study ten matches they play in and note down key aspects of their game and then apply it to your own tekkers!

Prep like a pro!
6 We're all up for a game of FIFA, but there's a time and place – and before a game is not the time. Get focused, fuel yourself properly and have a good warm-up!

Join a team!
7 You might look like a baller in your garden, but it only counts on the pitch. Join a local team and show off your tekkers when it really matters. It'll feel ledge!

Use your voice!
8 Don't be afraid to tell your team-mates how it is in a constructive way. Top players talk to each other on the pitch and offer helpful tactical tips!

Set yourself goals!
9 How are you supposed to kick on with your footy without ambition? Set yourself season targets, whether it's goals, assists or starts in the team, and do everything you can to reach them!

11

Recover right!
MAKE SURE YOU drink plenty of water after training and matches, and get lots of rest. You won't be at your best next game if you don't!

Stay motivated!
13 Without that, you won't be able to play to the best of your ability. If you want to make it to the top you need to WANT to be out there, giving it your all. So never lose sight of what your targets are!

Just give two-footed tackles a miss!

14

10

Find your signature!
ALL TOP players have a special move. Mesut Ozil loves assisting and Arjen Robben cuts inside. Discover yours and it'll give you an edge over other players!

Understand what it takes!
 12 This part is huge! You'll never become a pro baller without learning about how to get there. Following all of MOTD mag's Tekkers page tips is a good start!

Become two-footed!
NEED PROOF THAT two-footed ballers are better than one? Look no further than Lionel Messi, readers. He causes chaos and defenders never know which way he'll go!

TURN OVER FOR MORE!

15

Kit yourself out!

Sick ballers need sick gear! Save up your pocket money and net some swazzy training garms and a pair of decent shinnies!

Find a mentor!

20 Everyone needs a kick up the butt every now and then. Find someone who'll keep you focused, give you good advice and who you can talk footy with. It helps to have someone to turn to!

Remember it's a team game!

21 With some practise and the right attitude, you'll become a baller in no time – but you need to remember it's not just about you. It's about the team and winning. That's where the real ballers are at!

Take your chances!

22 Don't turn down a good opportunity because you're nervous – only if it doesn't seem right for you. You never know where something might lead!

Get match fit!

16 You might feel fit running around with your pals, but in-game fitness is a whole new ball game. The only way you can get match fit? By playing matches!

Know the rules!

17 The last thing you want is to mess up over a silly rule during a match. It might sound simple, but learn ALL footy rules and it'll help you lead by example!

Challenge yourself!

18 Don't stay in your comfort zone. If matches are too easy, step up and move to a better team and test your ability!

19

Prevent injuries!

WARMING UP AND down before and after games will keep your muscles in good shape. If you feel pain, don't play through it. Rest up and get it looked at. Don't cause any long-term damage!

It's gotta be done, readers

Don't let the pressure of a big game get to you!

 23

Perform when it matters!

IF A CHANCE falls to you in the box, make it count. Ronaldo always turns up for the big moments in big games. Be the match-winner everyone remembers!

 26
Turn up the tricks!
Every top baller needs to have some well silky skills in their locker! Flashes of magic on the pitch always catch people's attention – and you just never know who could be watching!

 29
Be a leader!
Talk to your team-mates and be a leader on the pitch! All the best ballers are looked up to by their squad – and you need to earn that respect!

24

Add some swaz!
THERE'S NOTHING WRONG with a smidge of swaz every now and again. Not every ball has to be delicately chipped. Swaz the leather off it and turn some heads, yeah?

 27
Be patient!
Don't beat yourself up if you haven't been playing well. Your form will pick up eventually – just keep practising and training well. Hard work beats talent – because sometimes talent isn't enough!

28
Perfect your touch!
You'll be surprised how many tough situations a good first touch can get you out of. Work on controlling the ball in pressured, tight situations and you'll be the team's go-to composure king!

 **30**

Become a winner!
DON'T SETTLE FOR anything other than a win! C-Ron lives his life this way and so should you. Do whatever it takes for you to come out on top!

 25
Deal with nerves!
Those butterflies are actually your body's way of confronting your fears. Identify what's making you feel nervous and build a plan to push past it. Plus, never confuse nerves with excitement!

10 BIGGEST FOOT

2 WEMBLEY STADIUM
90,000
LOCATION: LONDON, ENGLAND
BUILT: 2007
HOME OF: ENGLAND & TOTTENHAM 2017-18

4 STADE DE FRANCE
81,338
LOCATION: PARIS, FRANCE
BUILT: 1998
HOME OF: FRANCE

9 OLD TRAFFORD
75,635
LOCATION: MANCHESTER, ENGLAND
BUILT: 1910
HOME OF: MAN. UNITED

6 SANTIAGO BERNABEU
81,044
LOCATION: MADRID, SPAIN
BUILT: 1947
HOME OF: REAL MADRID

1 NOU CAMP
99,354
LOCATION: BARCELONA, SPAIN
BUILT: 1957
HOME OF: BARCELONA

STADIUMS IN EUROPE!

3 WESTFALENSTADION

81,359

LOCATION: DORTMUND, GERMANY

BUILT: 1974

HOME OF: BORUSSIA DORTMUND

7 LUZHNIKI STADIUM

81,000

LOCATION: MOSCOW, RUSSIA

BUILT: 1956

HOME OF: RUSSIA

10 ALLIANZ ARENA

75,000

LOCATION: MUNICH, GERMANY

BUILT: 2005

HOME OF: BAYERN MUNICH & 1860 MUNICH

8 ATATURK OLYMPIC STADIUM

76,092

LOCATION: ISTANBUL, TURKEY

BUILT: 2001

HOME OF: TURKEY

5 SAN SIRO

81,227

LOCATION: MILAN, ITALY

BUILT: 1926

HOME OF: AC MILAN & INTER MILAN

EDINSON CAVANI

PSG

THE ULTIMATE FAMILY FOOTY QUIZ!

Woof, woof!

You versus your dad or mum...
There can only be one winner...
But who will it be?

p84-87 A QUIZ FOR YOU p88-91 A QUIZ FOR YOUR DAD

TURN OVER NOW!

QUIZ FOR YOU!

10 points for each correct answer!

1 Which club have won the most Champions League titles?

A Real Madrid ✓ | **B AC Milan** ✓ | **C Liverpool** ✓ | **D Bayern Munich** ✓

2 Ernesto Valverde is the manager of Barcelona – but which one is he?

A ✓ | B ✓

C ✓ | D ✓

3 Which tournament did this England team compete at?

A World Cup 2010 ✓ | B Euro 2016 ✓
C World Cup 2014 ✓ | D Euro 2012 ✓

4 With which club did Romelu Lukaku start his career?

A Chelsea ✓ | B Club Brugge ✓
C Anderlecht ✓ | D Genk ✓

5 Which of these is Bayern Munich and Germany star Joshua Kimmich?

A ✓ | B ✓

C ✓ | D ✓

6
2017 UCL final goalscorer Mario Mandzukic plays for which country?

A Serbia	B Russia
C Croatia	D Hungary

7
Which League Two club is nicknamed The Grecians?

A Port Vale	B Yeovil
C Grimsby	D Exeter

8
Which European club plays at the Stade Velodrome?

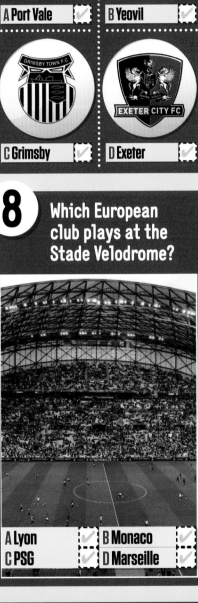

A Lyon	B Monaco
C PSG	D Marseille

9
Which of these players has the most caps for Spain?

A Gerard Pique

B Sergio Busquets

C Juan Mata

D David Silva

10
Who won last season's FA Cup?

 A Chelsea

 B Arsenal

 C Tottenham

 D Man. City

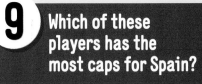
HOW DID YOU DO? TURN TO p92 FOR THE ANSWERS!

Your total ☐/100

TURN OVER FOR MORE!

QUIZ FOR YOU!

SECOND HALF!

10 points for each correct answer!

11 Which of these shirts belongs to Atletico Madrid?

A
B
C
D

12 Name this world-famous stadium!

A The Emirates
B Wembley
C Old Trafford
D Anfield

14 Who is this Premier League referee?

A Michael Oliver
B Mike Dean
C Anthony Taylor
D Martin Atkinson

13 Which of these players was top scorer at Euro 2016?

A Griezmann
B Ronaldo
C Payet
D Bale

15 Who did Man. United beat in last season's Europa League final?

A Celta Vigo
B Ajax
C Wolfsburg
D Lyon

16
From which club did Chelsea sign Eden Hazard?

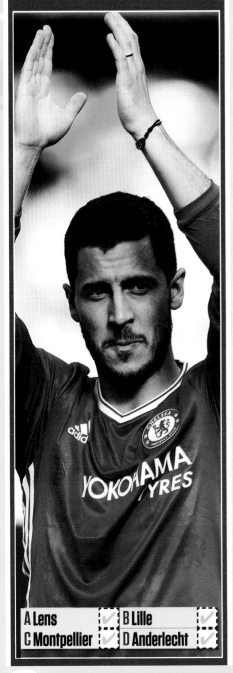

A Lens
B Lille
C Montpellier
D Anderlecht

17
Which Italian team is lining up in this photo below?

A Sampdoria
B Inter Milan
C Brescia
D Atalanta

18
Which of these has scored the most Prem career goals?

A Crouch

B Kane

C Walcott

D Sturridge

19
Which of these is Bournemouth ace Steve Cook?

A

B

C

D

20
Norrkoping and AIK are teams from which country?

A Iceland
B Denmark
C Sweden
D Norway

HOW DID YOU DO?
TURN TO p92 FOR THE ANSWERS!

Your total
☐ /200

TURN OVER FOR MORE!

QUIZ FOR YOUR DAD!

10 points for each correct answer!

FIRST HALF!

1 Which club won the first Premier League title in 1992-93?

A Blackburn ✓

B Leeds ✓

C Man. United ✓

D Arsenal ✓

2 This man became a legend at which tournament?

A Mexico 86 ✓ B Italia 90 ✓
C USA 94 ✓ D France 98 ✓

3 Brian Deane scored the first Prem goal. Tick the player you think he is!

 A ✓
 B ✓
 C ✓
 D ✓

4 Dion Dublin was joint-top scorer in the Prem in 1997-98 – but for which club?

A Man. United ✓
B Aston Villa ✓
C Coventry ✓
D Leeds ✓

5 Who managed Everton to FA Cup success in 1994-95?

A Howard Kendall ✓

B Joe Royle ✓

C David Moyes ✓

D Walter Smith ✓

6

1997 UCL winner Stephane Chapuisat played for which international team?

A France	B Switzerland
C Austria	D Denmark

7

Who managed England at the 1992 European Championships?

A Bobby Robson

B Terry Venables

C Howard Wilkinson

D Graham Taylor

8

Which European team is this lining up for a Champions League clash?

A Inter Milan	B Juventus
C Real Madrid	D Marseille

9

Which of these players is Serie A goalscoring legend Enrico Chiesa?

A

B

C

D

10

Which of these countries won Euro 2000?

A Italy   B Germany   C France   D Greece

HOW DID YOU DO?
TURN TO p92 FOR THE ANSWERS!

Dad's total ☐/100

TURN OVER FOR MORE!

QUIZ FOR YOUR DAD!

10 points for each correct answer!

11 Which of these clubs did Paul Gascoigne finish his career at?

A Burnley ✓ | B Middlesbrough ✓ | C Boston ✓ | D Everton ✓

12 Which of these is ex-Blackburn & England winger Stuart Ripley?

A ✓ | B ✓

C ✓ | D ✓

13 Which club used to play at Roker Park?

A Bolton ✓ | B Sunderland ✓
C Middlesbrough ✓ | D Derby ✓

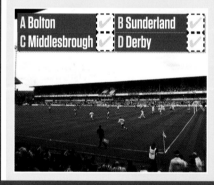

14 Which player once famously pushed referee Paul Alcock to the floor?

A Neil Ruddock ✓
B Paolo Di Canio ✓
C Roy Keane ✓
D Vinnie Jones ✓

15 Brazil striker Bebeto was a star at USA 94 – which one is he?

A ✓ | B ✓

C ✓ | D ✓

16 Which Italian team did ex-England midfielder Paul Ince play for?

A AC Milan ☑

B Inter Milan ☑

C Napoli ☑

D Sampdoria ☑

17 Which nation hosted the 1992 Euros, won by Denmark?

A Denmark ☑   B Germany ☑
C Sweden ☑   D England ☑

18 Which country did 1990s baller Hristo Stoichkov play for?

A Bulgaria ☑   B Romania ☑
C Russia ☑   D Hungary ☑

19 Who has played more times for England?

A Frank Lampard ☑

B Rio Ferdinand ☑

C Ashley Cole ☑

D Gary Neville ☑

20 Which of these players was top scorer at the France 98 World Cup?

A Davor Suker ☑

B Gabriel Batistuta ☑

C Ronaldo ☑

D Thierry Henry ☑

HOW DID YOU DO?
TURN TO p92 FOR THE ANSWERS!

Dad's total
☐ /200

QUIZ ANSWERS!

QUIZ 1 FROM PAGE 12
FOOTY DETECTIVE QUIZ ANSWERS
LEAGUE A MLS
LEAGUE B La Liga
LEAGUE C Argentine Premier League
LEAGUE D Bundesliga

MY SCORE [ANSWER] OUT OF 4

QUIZ 2 FROM PAGE 28
EURO GIANTS CROSSWORD ANSWERS

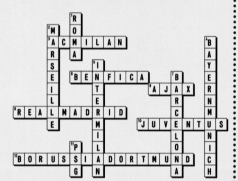

Crossword answers:
MARSEILLE, ROMA, AC MILAN, INTER MILAN, BENFICA, AJAX, BAYERN MUNICH, REAL MADRID, JUVENTUS, PSG, BORUSSIA DORTMUND, BARCELONA

MY SCORE [ANSWER] OUT OF 12

QUIZ 3 FROM PAGE 36
WHO'S THE OLDEST ANSWERS
1 Luis Suarez
2 Laurent Koscielny
3 Gonzalo Higuain
4 Ander Herrera
5 Jamie Vardy
6 Daniel Sturridge
7 Tom Heaton
8 Mesut Ozil
9 Pep Guardiola

MY SCORE [ANSWER] OUT OF 9

KING LUIS Yep – he's older than Messi!

TOP GUNS Arsenal beat Chelsea 2-1 in the 2016-17 FA Cup final!

QUIZ 4 FROM PAGE 44
THE COUNTRY QUIZ ANSWERS
1 B Austria
2 B Croatia
3 A Germany
4 A Holland
5 B Bolivia
6 A Brazil
7 B Chile
8 A Australia
9 A France

MY SCORE [ANSWER] OUT OF 9

QUIZ 5 FROM PAGE 73
A YEAR IN FOOTBALL ANSWERS
1 B Tottenham
2 B Arsenal 2-1 Chelsea
3 C Leicester
4 B Lincoln
5 C Man. United
6 A Lionel Messi
7 B Cristano Ronaldo
8 A Bayer Leverkusen
9 B Granada

MY SCORE [ANSWER] OUT OF 9

THE ULTIMATE FAMILY FOOTY QUIZ FROM PAGE 83
QUIZ FOR YOU ANSWERS
1 A Real Madrid
2 A
3 C World Cup 2014
4 C Anderlecht
5 D
6 C Croatia
7 D Exeter

8 D Marseille
9 D David Silva
10 B Arsenal
11 C
12 A The Emirates
13 A Antoine Griezmann
14 A Michael Oliver
15 B Ajax
16 B Lille
17 A Sampdoria
18 A Peter Crouch
19 C
20 C Sweden

MY SCORE [ANSWER] OUT OF 200

QUIZ FOR DAD ANSWERS
1 C Man. United
2 B Italia 90
3 A
4 C Coventry
5 B Joe Royle
6 B Switzerland
7 D Graham Taylor
8 B Juventus
9 A
10 C France
11 C Boston
12 B
13 B Sunderland
14 B Paolo Di Canio
15 B
16 B Inter Milan
17 C Sweden
18 A Bulgaria
19 C Ashley Cole
20 A Davor Suker

MY SCORE [ANSWER] OUT OF 200

MATCH of the DAY

Kane

Ozil

The F2

THE BIGGEST SUPERSTARS EVERY WEEK!

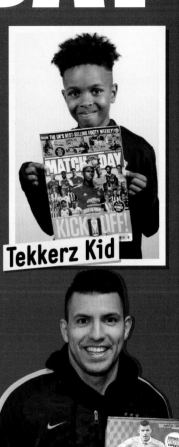

Tekkerz Kid

Aguero

THE UK'S BEST-SELLING FOOTY MAG!

MATCH of the DAY

Write to us at
Match of the Day magazine
Immediate Media, Vineyard House,
44 Brook Green, Hammersmith,
London, W6 7BT

Telephone 020 7150 5513
Email shout@motdmag.com
pazandketch@motdmag.com
motdmag.com

Match Of The Day editor	Ian Foster	Production editor	Neil Queen-Jones
Annual editor	Mark Parry	Deputy production editor	Joe Shackley
Senior art editor	Blue Buxton	Publishing consultant	Jaynie Bye
Designers	Al Parr, Rod Edwards, Pete Rogers	Editorial director	Corinna Shaffer
		Annual images	Getty Images
News editor	Matthew Ketchell		
Senior writer	Lee Stobbs		
Group picture editor	Natasha Thompson		

BBC Books, an imprint of Ebury Publishing, 20 Vauxhall Bridge Road, London SW1V 2SA. BBC Books is part of the Penguin Random House group of companies whose addresses can be found at global.penguinrandomhouse.com. Copyright © Match Of The Day magazine, 2017. First published by BBC Books in 2017. www.penguin.co.uk. A CIP catalogue record for this book is available from the British Library. ISBN 9781785942051. Commissioning editor: Albert DePetrillo; project editor: Benjamin McConnell; production: Phil Spencer. Printed and bound in Italy by Rotolito Lombarda SpA. Penguin Random House is committed to a sustainable future for our business, our readers and our planet. This book is made from Forest Stewardship Council ® certified paper.

BBC

The licence to publish this magazine was acquired from BBC Worldwide by Immediate Media Company on 1 November 2011. We remain committed to making a magazine of the highest editorial quality, one that complies with BBC editorial and commercial guidelines and connects with BBC programmes.

Match Of The Day Magazine is is published by Immediate Media Company London Limited, under licence from BBC Worldwide Limited. © Immediate Media Company London Limited, 2017.

FAKE NEWS

What do you mean these stories, aren't true

Fake news!

OOH, LOOK – a hairy, scary beast... and the Gruffalo

OH NO, IT'S THE G-ROO-FFALO

WAYNE ROONEY is the long-lost brother of the Gruffalo, we can exclusively reveal.

Scientists from Switzerland examining new DNA evidence made the shocking discovery at a top-secret lab in the Deep Dark Wood on Wednesday.

Rooney, who met his sibling for the first time this morning, said: "Gruff's cool. His eyes are orange, his tongue is black, he has purple prickles all over his back."

CRISP-IANO'S CHEESY SECRET

MALCOLM would literally lick anything – the weirdo

CRISTIANO RONALDO tastes like a cheesy Wotsit, it was sensationally claimed last night.

Football nut Malcolm Spratt, from Huddersfield, says he licked the Real Madrid man's face after bumping into him in a hotel lobby last week.

Mr Spratt, 47, said: "It were just like licking a big Wotsit – you know, the cheesy corn snack that turns your fingers bright orange. I love Wotsits, me."